Enjoy-
Maggie

MAGGIE'S IRELAND

 BOOKS

Maggie's Ireland
PUBLISHED BY XRX BOOKS

PUBLISHER
Alexis Yiorgos Xenakis

MANAGING EDITOR
David Xenakis

EDITOR
Elaine Rowley

EDITORIAL ASSISTANT
Sue Nelson

INSTRUCTION ASSISTANTS
Cole Kelley
Teri Roberts

COPY EDITOR
Holly Brunner

GRAPHIC DESIGNER
Bob Natz

PHOTOGRAPHER
Alexis Xenakis

SECOND PHOTOGRAPHER
Mike Winkleman

PHOTO STYLIST
Rick Mondragon

PRODUCTION DIRECTOR & COLOR SPECIALIST
Dennis Pearson

BOOK PRODUCTION MANAGER
Nancy Steers

PRODUCTION
Everett Baker
Nancy Holzer

TECHNICAL ILLUSTRATIONS
Jay Reeve
Carol Skallerud

SPECIAL ILLUSTRATIONS
Natalie Sorenson

MIS
Jason Bittner

FIRST PUBLISHED IN USA IN 2004 BY XRX, INC.

COPYRIGHT © 2004 XRX, INC.

ISBN 1-8937621-8-1

Produced in Sioux Falls, South Dakota, by XRX, Inc.,
PO Box 1525, Sioux Falls, SD 57101-1525 USA
605.338.2450

another publication of XX BOOKS

Visit us online at www.knittinguniverse.com

MAGGIE'S IRELAND

DESIGNER KNITS
ON LOCATION

Collection by Maggie Jackson
Photography by Alexis Xenakis

MAGGIE'S IRELAND

Front cover *Carrick-a-rede Rope Bridge*
Front end paper *Mussenden Temple*
Photo pages, ii *Archway, Devenish Island*
iv *Sheep in the Mourne Mountains*
vi *Giant's Causeway*
viii *Devenish Island*
x *Ballintoy Harbor*
xii *Ulster Folk and Transport Museum*
Above *Ireland panorama*
Back end paper *Grianán of Aligh*
Back cover *Dunluce Castle*

CONTENTS

Simply beautiful, simply done . . .
It's easy!

At first glance, these garments appear to be a knitting challenge. In fact, they are interesting knitting but not at all difficult.

Simple stitches are worked into blocks and bands of texture; stitch markers and color-coded drawings keep it easy.

Color is added one yarn at a time. After a split or tube is worked, that yarn ends and you pick up the next one (see how, on the following pages). Occasionally a mixture of yarns is transformed into one wonderful hand-knotted strand, or made into tassels that stack to form a ruff.

Maggie combines and recombines these signature elements in ways that make each project fun to knit and the entire collection a stimulating source of ideas.

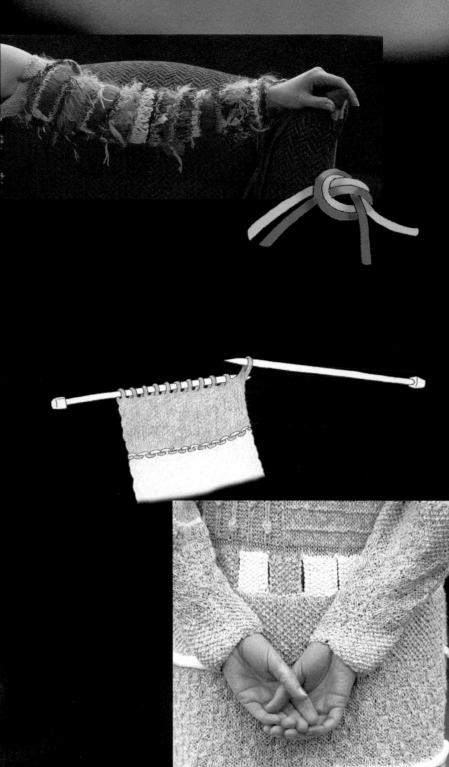

Splits — Tubes — *It's easy!* — Square Knot

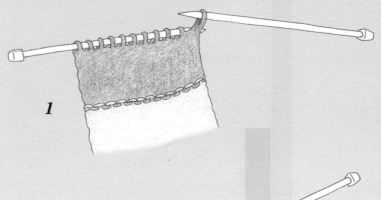

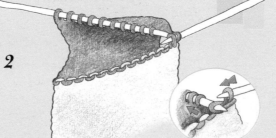

1

2

3

SPLITS are an easy way to mix yarns, colors, and stitch patterns across a piece of knitting.
1 Work back and forth across a few stitches (number and length specified in the pattern), ending with a right-side row and leaving stitches on right-hand needle: one section completed. Cut yarn. Work next section to same length. (Depending on yarn and stitch, this could require more rows or fewer rows than the last section). Drawing shows two sections completed and a third in process.
2, 3 Sew each section to next section at top and bottom with a couple of stitches to neaten and secure, then weave in ends.

2

3

TUBE
Beginning with a RS row, work 7 rows Stockinette stitch (k on RS, p on WS) (9 rows for kid's garments).
1 **Close Tube** Turn work (WS facing): * Slip 1 stitch from left-hand (LH) needle to right-hand (RH) needle.
2 Insert RH needle under strand running between first stitch and second stitch on first row of Tube.
3 Slip stitch on RH needle over strand; continue from * across Tube stitches.
At end of row, slip last stitch on LH needle to RH needle.
Next row (RS) Work as directed in pattern.

NOTE
If Tube yarn is similar in color to main yarn, knit first row of Tube with Tube yarn and a contrast thread. Pull out contrast thread after closing Tube.

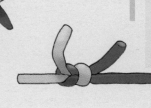

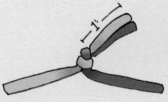

Overhand knot

Hand-knotted rag yarn

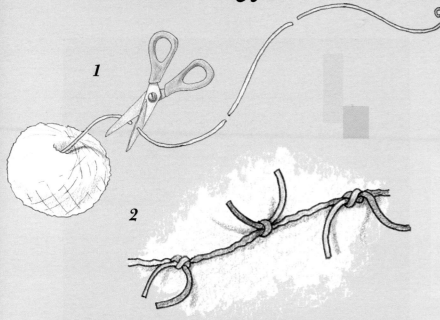

1 Cut yarn into lengths as stated in pattern.
2 Knot together, leaving tails of approximately 1".
Use either a square knot or overhand knot.
Cut and knot as you go, or prepare the hand-knotted
yarn before you knit.

Rag Mix Assorted yarns are cut then knotted in
sequence.

Make tassels

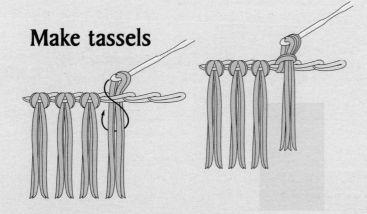

1 Cut lengths of yarn and fold.
2 Insert crochet hook through a stitch.
3 Draw fold through fabric (stitch), forming a loop.
4 Draw ends through loop.

Measure & cut elastic

1

1 Measure above bust and
at top of arm.
2 Cut elastic 2–3" shorter
than measurements.

Sew elastic

Overlap ends of elastic by ½"
and sew with double thread.

Insert elastic

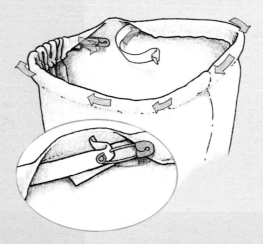

1 Sew casing, leaving a small opening.
2 Insert elastic using a safety pin or bodkin.
3 Overlap ends of elastic and sew together.
4 Finish seaming casing shut.

Simple seams

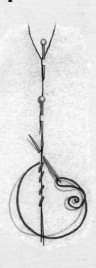

Use a flat seam to reduce bulk.
1 Pin edges together.
2 Seam with whip stitch.

SECTION 1 HINTS OF WHITE

Yarns

- **L** natural linen
- **R** ivory ribbon
- **C** cream linen

Stitches

- Stockinette
- Seed
- Basket Weave
- SRS
- P5, K1 Rib
- Tube
- Split

His Sweater

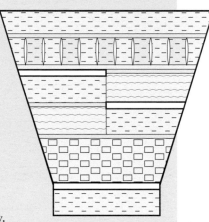

LOOSE FIT

Skill Intermediate

Fit Loose

Size S (M, L, 1X)

Approximate measurements

A 42 (44, 47, 50)"

B 28 (29, 29, 29)"; optional: make Back 2" longer

C 30 (30, 29, 29)

Gauge 18 sts and 24 rows to 10cm/4" over Seed st with L

Yarn Medium weight

L 1500 (1600, 1700, 1800) yds linen blend

R 95 yds ribbon

C 125 yds linen blend

Needles 5mm/US8, or size to obtain gauge

Extras Markers, matching thread

STOCKINETTE STITCH
(St st)
RS rows Knit.
WS rows Purl.

SEED STITCH
Row 1 * K1, p1; repeat from *.
Row 2 P the knit sts and k the purl sts.
Repeat Row 2 for Seed st.

BASKET WEAVE
Row 1 (RS) * K4, p4; repeat from *.
Rows 2–4 K the knit sts and p the purl sts.
Row 5 * P4, k4; repeat from *.
Rows 6–8 K the knit sts and p the purl sts.
Repeat Rows 1–8.

SINGLE RIDGE STITCH
(SRS)
Rows 1 and 3 (RS) Knit.
Rows 2 and 4 (WS) Purl.
Rows 5 and 6 Purl.
Rows 7 and 9 Knit.
Row 8 Purl.
Row 10 Knit.
Repeat Rows 1–10.

P5, K1 RIB
RS rows * P5, k1; repeat from *.
WS rows K the knit sts and p the purl sts.

TUBE
Beginning with a RS row, work 7 rows in St st.
Close Tube Turn work (WS facing): * Slip 1 st from left-hand (LH) needle to right-hand (RH) needle; insert RH needle under strand running between first st and second st on first row of Tube; slip st on RH needle over strand; continue from * across Tube sts. At end of row, slip last st on LH needle to RH needle.

NOTES
1 See *It's Easy*, page 1, for Tubes and Splits. **2** End each pattern-stitch section with a wrong-side (WS) row, unless directed to end with a right-side (RS) row. **3** When changing colors, bring new color under old color to prevent holes, and work first row in St st.

His Sweater
SLEEVES
With L, cast on 44 (46, 48, 50) sts. Work Seed st for 3".
Increasing Increase 1 st at beginning and end of every RS row 15 (14, 13, 12) times—74 sts on needle. Then increase every other RS row to top of sleeve (do not increase on Tube rows). AT SAME TIME, work patterns and yarns as follows:
Tube With C, work Tube over all sts.
Next 4" With L, work Basket Weave.
Next 2 rows With R, work St st.
Next row (RS) Mark center of row. With L, work Seed st to center of row, work SRS to end of row. Work pattern for 4 (4, 3, 3)".
Next row (RS) With C, work Tube to center of row; with L, k Tube sts; with R, k to end.
Next row (WS) With R, purl R sts; with L, purl L sts.
Next row (RS) With L, work SRS to center of row, work Seed st to end of row. Work pattern for 4 (3, 3, 3)".
Next row (RS) With R, k to center; with C, work Tube over remaining sts; join L, k Tube sts.
Next row (WS) With L, purl L sts; with R, purl R sts.
Next 2 rows With L, work St st.
2" Seed-st Splits Mark center 90 sts. With L, work Seed st to center sts, turn, work Seed st back and

forth on edge sts for 2", ending with a RS row (Seed-st section); with R, work Seed-st section on center 10 sts; with L, work Seed-st section on next 10 sts; continue across remaining sts, alternately working 10-st sections in R and in L; with L, work edge section on remaining sts.
Next row (WS) With L, purl.
Next 2 rows With R, work St st.
Next 2" With L, work Seed st. Bind off loosely.

FRONT AND BACK
With L, cast on 94 (100, 106, 112) sts.
Work Seed st for 3".
Next row (RS) Knit, increasing by k into front and back of every 10th st —103 (110, 116, 123) sts.
Next row (WS) Purl.
Next row (RS) With C, work 40 (44, 48, 52)-st Tube; with L, k Tube sts and work Basket Weave to end of row.
Next 4" Beginning with a WS row, continue Basket Weave over all sts.
Next row (RS) With L, k to last 40 (44, 48, 52) sts; with C, work 40 (44, 48, 52)-st Tube; with L, k Tube sts.
Next 3" Beginning with a WS row, with L, work Seed st.
Next 2 rows With R, work St st.
2" Seed-st Splits With L, work 16 (20, 23, 26)-st section; work 10-st sections in: L, L, R, L, R, L, L; with L, work 17 (20, 23, 27)-st section.
Next row (WS) With L, purl.
Next 2 rows With R, work St st.

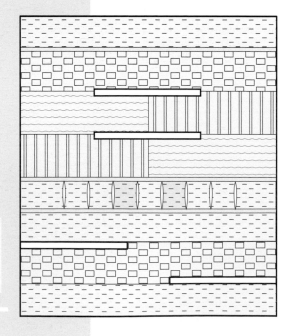

Next row (RS) With L, work 51 (55, 58, 61) sts SRS; work 52 (55, 58, 62) sts P5, K1 Rib. Work pattern for 4".

* **Next row** (RS) With L, k to center 50 sts; with C, work 50-st Tube; with L, k Tube sts and k to end of row.

Next row (WS) Purl. *

Next row (RS) Work 51 (55, 58, 61) sts P5, K1 Rib, work 52 (55, 58, 62) sts SRS. Work pattern for 4".

Repeat from * to *.

Next 3 (4, 4, 4)" Work Basket Weave.

Next 2 rows With R, work St st.

Next row (RS) With L, knit.

Next 3 (4, 4, 4)" Beginning with a WS row, work Seed st. (Adjust length if desired, but work no less than 1" Seed st.)

Bind off loosely.

MAKING UP

Secure Splits (see page 1). Secure ends of ribbon with thread. Sew shoulder seams, leaving approximately 12" open at center. Sew Sleeves to body, centering at shoulder seam. Sew Sleeve and side seams, above top of first Seed-st band on Front. Press seams lightly using damp cloth.

His Sweater 12 (13, 14, 15) balls MAGGI'S LINEN (L) in Natural; 1 ball each: MAGGI'S RIBBON (R) in Ivory, MAGGI'S LINEN in Cream (C)

Yarns

- **L** *natural linen*
- **W** *white linen*
- **S** *silver metallic*
- **R** *white ribbon*

Stitches

- *Stockinette*
- *Seed*
- *SRS*
- *Basket Weave*
- *AB Rib*
- *P5, K1 Rib*
- *Tube*
- *Split*

Her Sweater

LOOSE FIT

Skill Intermediate

Fit Loose

Size S (M, L)

Approximate measurements

A 40 (43½, 47)

B 28 (29, 29)"; optional: make Back 2"
longer

C 29"

Gauge 18 sts and 24 rows to 10cm/4" over
Seed st with L

Yarn Medium weight

L 1400 (1550, 1700) yds linen blend

W 125 yds linen blend

S 85 yds metallic

R 95 yds ribbon

Needles 5mm/US8, or size to obtain gauge

Extras Markers, matching thread

ALTERNATING BOBBLE RIB (AB RIB)

Row 1 (RS) * P5, k1; repeat from *.

Rows 2–4 K the knit sts and p the purl sts.

Row 5 P5, * work Bobble [(p1, k1, p1, k1) in next st, turn, k4, turn, p4], p5, k1, p5; repeat from *.

Row 6 K the knit sts and p the purl sts EXCEPT p the 4 Bobble sts together.

Rows 7–10 Repeat Rows 1–4.

Row 11 P5, k1, p5, * work Bobble in next st, p5, k1, p5, repeat from *.

Row 12 Repeat Row 6.

Repeat Rows 1–12.

STOCKINETTE, SEED, SRS, BASKET WEAVE, P5, K1 RIB, & TUBE

See page 6.

NOTES

1 See *It's Easy*, page 1, for Tubes & Splits. *2* End each pattern-stitch section with a wrong-side (WS) row, unless directed to end with a right-side (RS) row. *3* When changing colors, work first row in St st.

Her Sweater
RIGHT SLEEVE

* With L, cast on 44 (46, 48) sts. Work Seed st for 3".

Increasing Increase 1 st at beginning and end of every RS row 15 (14, 13) times—74 sts on needle. Then increase every other RS row to top of sleeve. (Do not increase on Tube rows). AT SAME TIME, work patterns and yarns as follows:

Next 5 (4, 4)" With L, work Basket Weave. *

Work St st 2 rows R, 2½" L, 2 rows S.

** 2" Seed-st Splits Mark center 10 sts. With L, work Seed st to center sts, turn, work Seed st back and forth on edge sts for 2", ending with a RS row (10-st Seed-st section); with R, work Seed-st section on center 10 sts; with L, work Seed-st section on remaining sts.

Next row (WS) With L, purl. **

Next 3" Work St st.

Tube With W, work Tube over all sts.

Next row (WS) With L, purl.

< Next 3 (3, 2)" Work Seed st to center 35 sts, work 35 sts AB Rib, work Seed st to end of row.

Next 1" Work Seed st.

Bind off loosely. >

LEFT SLEEVE

Work as Right Sleeve from * to *.
Work as Right Sleeve from ** to **, EXCEPT work 2 rows St st after Splits in S instead of 1 row in L.

Next 2" With L, work St st.

<<Next row (RS) With L, k to center 14 sts; with W, work 14-st Tube; with L, k Tube sts and to end of row.

Next 2" With L, work St st >>.
Repeat from << to >>.

Work as Right Sleeve from < to >.

FRONT

With L, cast on 94 (100, 106) sts. Work Seed st for 3".

Next row (RS) Knit, increasing by k into front and back of every 10th st—103 (110, 116) sts.

Next row (WS) Purl.

Next row (RS) With W, work 40 (44, 48)-st Tube; with L, k Tube sts to end of row.

Next row (WS) With L, purl.

Next 5" Work Basket Weave.

Next row (RS) With L, k to last 40 (44, 48) sts; with W work 40 (44, 48)-st Tube; with L, k Tube sts.

Next 3" Beginning with a WS row, with L, work Seed st.

Next 2 rows With R, work St st.

2" Seed-st Splits With L, work 16 (20, 23)-st section; work 10-st sections in L, R, R, L, R, L, R; with L, work 17 (20, 23)-st section.

Next row (WS) With L, purl.

Next 2 rows With S, work St st.

Next row (RS) With L, work 51 (55, 58) sts SRS; work 52 (55, 58) sts AB Rib. Work pattern for 6".

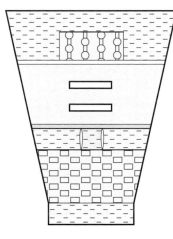

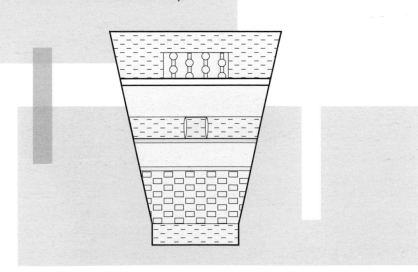

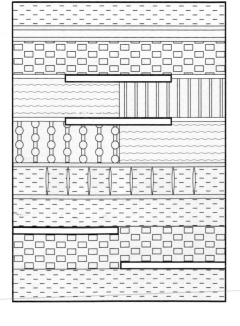

* Next row (RS) With W, k 26 (30, 33) sts, work 50-st Tube, k Tube sts and k to end of row.
Next row (WS) Purl. *
Next row (RS) With L, work 51 (55, 58) sts P5, K1 Rib, work 52 (55, 58) sts SRS. Work pattern for 4"
Repeat from * to *.
Next 3 (4, 4)" Work Basket Weave.
Work St st 2 rows R, 2 rows L, 2 rows R.
Next 1 (2, 2)" With L, work Seed st. (Adjust length if desired, but work no less than 1" Seed st.)
Bind off.

BACK
Work as Front. Or, to make Back 2" longer than Front, start with 4" Seed st rather than 3" and work Basket Weave for 6 (5, 5)" rather than 5 (4, 4)".

MAKING UP
Secure Splits (see page 1). Secure ends of ribbon with thread. Sew shoulder seams, leaving approximately 12" open at center. Sew Sleeves to body, centering at shoulder seam. Sew Sleeve and side seams, above top of first Seed-st band on Front. Press seams lightly using damp cloth.

Her Sweater 12 (13, 14) balls MAGGI'S LINEN (L) in Natural; 1 ball each: MAGGI'S RIBBON (R) in White, MAGGI'S LINEN in White (W); MAGGI'S METALLIC in Silver (S)

K2, P2 RIB
RS rows * K2, p2; repeat from *.
WS rows K the knit sts and p the purl sts.

BACK AND FRONT
Cast on 100 (110, 120) sts.
Work K2, P2 rib for 18" (knee-length) or 36" (full-length).
Next row (RS) Knit, working k2tog every 5th st—80 (88, 96) sts.

CASING
Next 7 rows Work St st (k on RS, p on WS).
Next row (RS) Purl.
Next 7 rows Work St st.
Bind off loosely.

MAKING UP
Sew side seams. Fold casing to WS along purl ridge and sew loosely, leaving an opening for elastic. Cut elastic 3" less than waist measurement. Thread elastic through opening, overlap ends by ½", and sew securely. Sew opening closed. Press seams lightly using a damp cloth.

A slip is recommended to be worn with this skirt.

Skirt

B | A

STANDARD FIT

Skill Easy
Fit Standard
Size S (M, L)
Approximate measurements
A 40 (44, 48)"
B Knee-length: 18"; full-length: 36"
Gauge 20 sts and 24 rows to 10cm/4" over
K2, P2 Rib with L, stretched slightly
Yarn Medium weight
L linen blend
Knee-length: 440 (490, 530) yds
Full-length: 895 (980, 1070) yds
Needles 4.5mm/US7, or size to obtain gauge
Extras 1 (1¼, 1¼) yd 1" elastic;
sewing thread

Skirt 8 (8, 9) balls MAGGI'S LINEN (L) in Natural for full-length skirt; 4 (4, 5) balls for knee-length skirt
Top left Botanic Doggy Coat (page 106) out for a stroll in the Botanic Gardens that border the University.

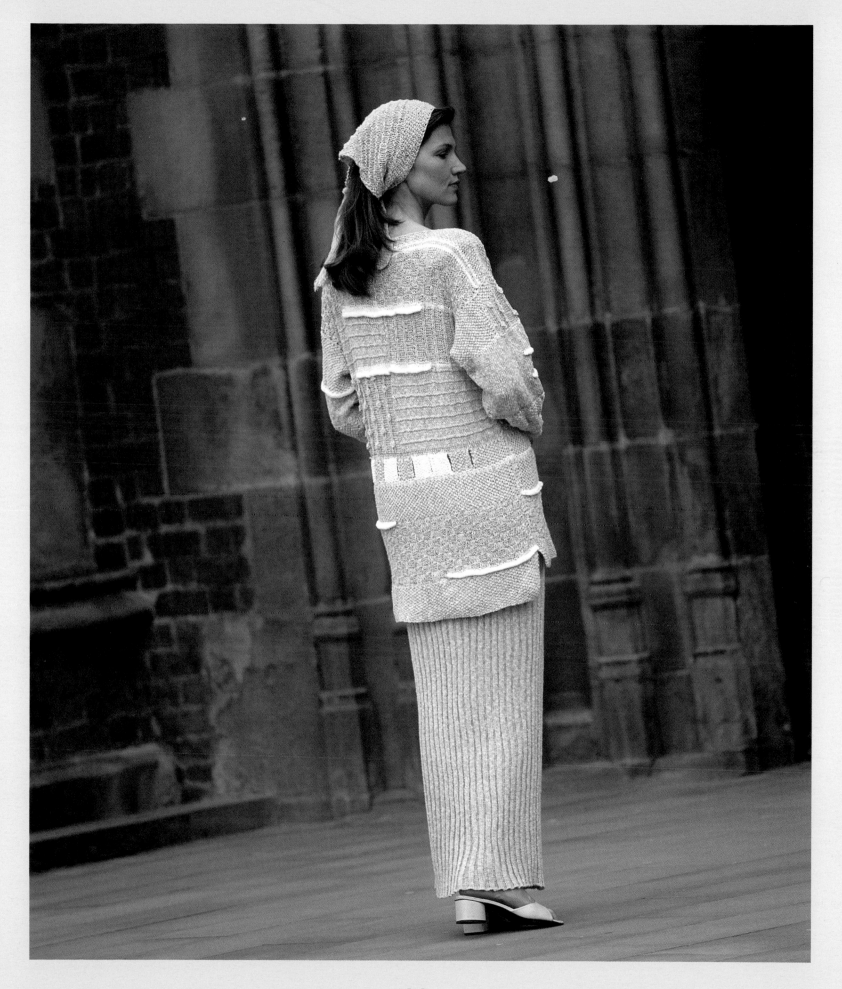

Ulster Folk and Transport Museum—a taste of the past.

CONNEMARA SWEATER

STOCKINETTE STITCH
(St st)
RS rows Knit.
WS rows Purl.

SEED STITCH
Row 1 (RS) * K1, p1; repeat from *.
Row 2 P the knit sts and k the purl sts.
Repeat Row 2 for Seed st.

LADDER STITCH
Row 1 (RS) Knit, wrapping yarn around the needle 3 times for every stitch (see page 170).
Row 2 Purl into sts, dropping wraps off needle.

NOTES
1 See *Techniques,* page 170, for working yarn overs between purl sts. *2* Use 2 strands of mohair (M) held together and 2 strands of linen (L) held together throughout. *3* End each pattern-stitch section with a wrong-side (WS) row. *4* When changing colors, work first row in St st.

Sweater
SLEEVES
With L, cast on 28 (30, 32) sts. Work 2" Seed st.
Begin increasing Increase 1 st at beginning and end of every 4th row (except Ladder-st rows) to top of Sleeve AT SAME TIME, work patterns and yarns as follows:
Continue Seed st until piece measures 6" from cast-on edge.
* Work 2 rows Ladder st.
Work St st [2 rows M, 2 rows L] 3 times; 2 rows M.
With L, work 2 rows Ladder st. *
With M, work Seed st until Sleeve measures 18 (17, 16)".
Bind off loosely.

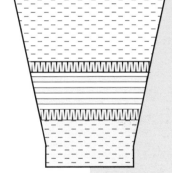

BACK AND FRONT
With L, cast on 68 (74, 80) sts.
Work 9" Seed st.
Work patterns and yarns as for Sleeve from * to *.
With M, work Seed st until piece measures 34" from beginning. (Shorten here if desired, be careful that Ladder st doesn't end up in an undesireable position.)
Bind off loosely.

MAKING UP
Sew shoulder seams, leaving approximately 11" open at center. Sew Sleeves to body, centering Sleeve at shoulder seam. Sew side seams, leaving bottom 7" open at both sides. Sew Sleeve seams.

COWL/HEADBAND
With 2 strands L held together, cast on 70 sts.
Work in Seed st for 6 to 7".
Bind off loosely.
Sew side seam.
To wear as headband, make a fold in back and fasten with a clip or decorative pin.

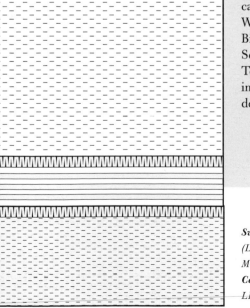

Sweater 6 (7, 7) balls MAGGI'S LINEN (L) in Natural; 8 (9, 9) balls MAGGI'S MOHAIR (M) in Ivory
Cowl or Headband 2 balls MAGGI'S LINEN in Natural

Yarns

M *ivory mohair*

L *natural linen*

Stitches

Stockinette

Seed

Ladder

LOOSE FIT

Skill Easy+
Fit Loose
Size S (M, L)
Approximate measurements
A 41 (45, 49)"
B 34"
C 28"
Gauge 13 stitches and 16 rows to 10cm/4" over Seed stitch with 2 strands of M
Yarn Medium weight
M 880 (990, 990) yds mohair
L 750 (880, 880) yds linen blend, add 250 yds for cowl/headband
Needles 6.5mm/US10½, or size to obtain gauge

Giant steps and wee blossoms along the Antrim Coast.

Yarns

☐ **M** ivory mohair

☐ **L** natural linen

Stitches

☐ Stockinette

▱ Seed

〰 Ladder

OVERSIZED FIT

Skill Easy+

Fit Oversized

Size S (M, L)

Approximate measurements

A 43 (47, 51)"

B 47 (49, 49)"

C 31"

Gauge 14 sts and 18 rows to 10cm/4" over St st with 2 strands of M

Yarn Medium weight

M 1320 (1540, 1760) yds mohair

L 1000 (1130, 1130) yds linen blend

Needles 6.5mm/US10½, or size to obtain gauge

STOCKINETTE STITCH

(St st)

RS rows Knit.

WS rows Purl.

SEED STITCH

Row 1 (RS) * K1, p1; repeat from *.

Row 2 P the knit sts and k the purl sts.

Repeat Row 2 for Seed st.

LADDER STITCH

Row 1 (RS) Knit, wrapping yarn around the needle 3 times for every stitch (see page 170).

Row 2 Purl into sts, dropping wraps off needle.

NOTES

1 Use 2 strands of mohair (M) held together and 2 strands of linen (L) held together throughout. *2* End each pattern-stitch section with a wrong-side (WS) row. *3* Coat can be made three-quarter length by working 2 to 3 fewer sections in Front and Back. *4* When changing colors, work first row in St st.

BACK

With M, cast on 72 (80, 88) sts.

Work 3" Seed st.

* With L, work 2 rows Ladder st.

Next row With M, work 10 sts Seed st, 52 (60, 68) sts St st, and 10 sts Seed st. Work as established for 3".

Repeat from * once more.

** With L, work 2 rows Ladder st, then 3" Seed st.

[With L, work 2 rows Ladder st. With M, work 4" St st] 2 times.

Repeat from ** once more.

With L, work 2 rows Ladder st, 2 (3, 3)" Seed st, and 2 rows Ladder st. (Adjust length in St st and Seed st areas here but work no less than 1" Seed st.)

With M, work 2" St st, then work 2" Seed st, AT SAME TIME, at beginning of last 2 rows, bind off 26 (30, 34) sts loosely.

Bind off remaining sts.

SLEEVES

With M, cast on 56 (58, 60) sts.

Work 3" Seed st.

With L, work 2 rows Ladder st.

Begin increasing Increase 1 st at beginning and end of every 6th row (except Ladder-st rows) to top of sleeve AT SAME TIME work patterns and yarns as follows:

* With M, work 3" St st. With L, work 2 rows Ladder st. *

** With L, work Seed st for 3". Work 2 rows Ladder st. **

Repeat from * to * once more.

Repeat from ** to ** once more.

With M, work 2 (1, 1)" Seed st.

Bind off loosely.

Coat

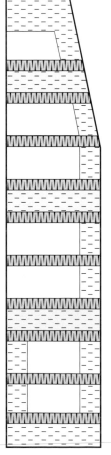

RIGHT FRONT

With M, cast on 38 (42, 46) sts.

Work 3" Seed st.

* With L, work 2 rows Ladder st.

Next row With M, work 10 sts Seed st, 18 (22, 26) sts St st, and 10 sts Seed st. Work as established for 3". *

Repeat from * to * once more.

With L, work 2 rows Ladder st.

Continue patterns and yarns as for Back, EXCEPT keep 10 sts at center front in Seed st in M sections, and AT SAME TIME, after 8th Ladder-st stripe, shape for neck: k2tog at beginning of every 4th row on RS (except Ladder-st rows) 12 times. Work even on 26 (30, 34) sts until same length as Back. Bind off loosely.

LEFT FRONT

Work as Right Front but reverse neck shaping (by k2tog at end of row).

COLLAR

With L, cast on 8 sts. Work in Seed st as follows: Work 7" even. Increase 1 st at beginning of every 6th row 10 times—18 sts. Work 10 rows even.

K2tog at beginning of every 4th row 6 times—12 sts. Work 5" even.

Increase 1 st at beginning of every 4th row 6 times—18 sts. Work 10 rows even.

K2tog at beginning of every 6th row 10 times—8 sts. Work 7" even. Bind off loosely.

MAKING UP

Sew shoulder seams. Sew Sleeves to body, centering Sleeve at shoulder seam. Sew side seams, leaving open to top of Seed-st border. Sew Sleeve seams.

Turn cuff to RS at first Ladder-st row and secure with a couple of stitches at side seam and halfway around.

Sew Collar to neck, centering Collar at Back neck and stitching evenly around neck and down each Front. Press seams, Front edges, and Collar lightly, using a damp cloth.

Shoulder pads are recommended.

Coat 12 (14, 16) balls MAGGI'S MOHAIR (M) in Ivory; 8 (9, 9) balls MAGGI'S LINEN (L) in Natural
The Ardee Shell (page 146) is worn under the coat.

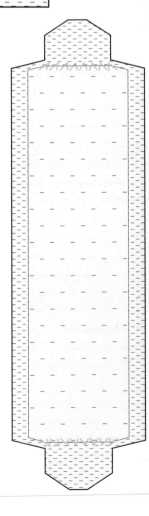

Stitches

 Stockinette

Seed

— Purl RS row

V Increase

Λ Decrease

Skirt

B | A
C
LOOSE FIT

Skill Intermediate

Fit Loose

Size S (M, L)

Approximate measurements

A 46 (49, 55½)"

B 38"

C 31 (33, 38½)"

Gauge 20 sts and 24 rows to 10cm/4" over St st

Yarn Medium weight

1260 (1380, 1510) yds linen blend

Needles 5mm/US 8, or size to obtain gauge

Extras Markers, crochet hook; ½" elastic for waist.

Shrug

Skill Intermediate

Fit Loose

Size One size

Approximate measurements 63" long, width at back 15"

Gauge 18 sts and 22 rows to 10cm/4" over Seed st

Yarn Medium weight

630 yds linen blend

Needles 5mm/US8, or size to obtain gauge

Extras Markers, crochet hook

STOCKINETTE STITCH

(St st)

RS rows Knit.

WS rows Purl.

SEED STITCH

Row 1 (RS) * K1, p1; repeat from *.

Row 2 P the knit sts and k the purl sts.

Repeat Row 2 for Seed st.

NOTES

1 See *Techniques,* page 170, for tassels. **2** End each pattern stitch section with a wrong-side (WS) row.

Skirt

BACK AND FRONT

With L, cast on 115 (123, 139) sts. Work 3" Seed st.

Begin borders Keeping 16 (14, 16) sts at beginning and end of every row in Seed st (place markers), work center 83 (95, 107) sts as follows:

Next 1" Work St st.

* **Tassel Row 1** [K11, p1] 6 (7, 8) times, k11.

Next 11 rows Work St st.

Tassel Row 2 K5, [p1, k11] 6 (7, 8) times, p1, k5.

Next 11 rows Work St st.

Repeat from * until piece measures 15" from beginning.

End borders Work St st across all sts, working Tassel Rows as follows:

Tassel Row 1 K3 (1, 3), [p1, k11] 9 (10, 11) times, p1, k3 (1, 3).

Tassel Row 2 K9 (7, 9), [p1, k11] 8 (9, 10) times, p1, k9 (7, 9).

Decrease within the pattern st on each Tassel Row 1 as follows:

First decrease row K3 (1, 3), [p2tog, k10] 9 (10, 11) times, p1, k3 (1, 3).

Next decrease row [P2tog, k9]. Continue thus, working a total of 4 decrease rows and working 1 fewer k st in repeat on each Tassel Row—79 (83, 95) sts.

Skirt is approximately 38" long; adjust length here if desired.

* **Next RS row** Purl.

Work 7 rows St st.

Repeat from * once. Bind off loosely.

ATTACHING TASSELS

Cut 24" length of L. Fold in half (12"), then in half again (6"). Working on RS of skirt piece, use crochet hook to pull loop through a purl st in a Tassel Row. Pull ends through loop and pull tight. Trim ends even. Add a tassel to every RS purl st in Tassel Rows.

MAKING UP

Sew side seams above Seed st. Fold waistband to WS at 2nd purl ridge and sew loosely, leaving an opening for elastic. Cut elastic 3" less than waist measurement. Thread elastic through opening, overlap ends by ½", and sew securely. Sew opening closed. Press seams lightly using a damp cloth.

Shrug
CUFF
Cast on 2 sts. Work Seed st,
increasing 1 st at beginning and
end of every row until 36 sts on
needle. Work even for 3".

TASSEL SECTION
Begin borders Keeping 10 sts at
beginning and end of every row in
Seed st (place markers) and work
center sts as follows:
Next row (RS) Knit in front and
back (kf&b) of next 16 sts—52 sts.
Next row P32.
Next row [Kf&b] 6 times, [k1,
kf&b] 10 times, [kf&b] 6 times—
74 sts.
Work 5 rows in St st.
* **Tassel Row 1** K10, [p1, k10] 4
times.
Next 11 rows Work St st.
Tassel Row 2 K4, [p1, k10] 4
times, p1, k5.
Next 11 rows Work St st.
Repeat from * until St st-section
measures approximately 56",
ending 3 rows after a tassel row.
Next row (RS) [K2tog] 6 times,
[k1, k2tog] 10 times, [k2tog] 6
times—52 sts. **Next row** Purl.
Next row [K2tog] 16 times—36 sts.

CUFF
Work Seed st for 3", then continue
in Seed st, decreasing 1 st each
end every row until 2 sts remain.
Bind off.

MAKING UP
Add tassels as for skirt.
Fold piece in half lengthwise and
seam cuff and continue for 15".
Press seams lightly using a damp
cloth.

*MAGGI'S LINEN in Natural: **Skirt** 10
(11, 12) balls; **Shrug** 5 balls
Nuala is wearing the Ardee top (page 146)
in Natural linen*

STOCKINETTE STITCH

(St st)
RS rows Knit.
WS rows Purl.

SEED STITCH

Row 1 * K1, p1; repeat from *.
Row 2 P the knit sts and k the purl sts.
Repeat Row 2 for Seed st.

LACY STITCH

All rows P1, * yo, p2tog; repeat from *, end p1.

NOTES

1 See *Techniques*, page 170, for cable cast on and working yarn overs between purl sts. **2** Work Sleeves from shoulder to cuff.

MAIN PIECE

With smaller needles cast on 4 sts.
Work in Seed st, increasing 1 st each end of every row to 22 sts.
Next row (RS) Work 8 sts Seed st, 6 sts St st, 8 sts Seed st.
Keeping 8-st Seed st border at beginning and end of every row (place markers), increase 1 st at beginning and end of St-st section every RS row (work increased sts in St st) until there are 78 St sts—94 sts total.
Next 10 rows Cable cast on 10 sts at beginning of row, work Seed st to marker, work 78 sts St st, work Seed st to end—194 sts.
Next 2 rows Cast on 10 (15, 20) sts, work Seed st to marker, dec 1 st in St-st section (k2tog on RS, p2tog on WS), work St st to 2 sts before second marker, dec 1 St st, work Seed st to end—210 (220, 230) sts.
Continue decreasing 1 st at markers every row, AT SAME TIME, work

10 additional sts in St st after second marker every row until only 8 sts at beginning and end of row remain in Seed st (border).
Keeping 8-st Seed-st borders, continue decreasing at markers every row until 166 (186, 206) sts remain.

Work even until skirt measures 17 (18, 18)" from last cast-on.
Waistband, next row (RS) Purl.
Next 6 rows Work St st.
Next row (WS) Knit.
Next 6 rows Work St st.
Bind off loosely.

FRILLS (make 3)

With smaller needles, cast on 130 sts.
Work Seed st for 1".
Next row K2tog across row—65 sts.
Bind off loosely.

LACY PIECES

Note With larger needles and 2 strands of linen held together, work Lacy st.
Large piece Cast on 6 sts.
Work 4 rows Lacy st.
* Cast on 2 sts at beginning of next 2 rows. Work 2 rows even. *
Repeat from * to * once more—14 sts.
** Cast on 4 sts at beginning of next 2 rows. Work 4 rows even.
Repeat from ** 3 more times—46 sts.
Repeat from * to * once more—50 sts.
Bind off 2 sts at beginning of every row 25 times. Fasten off.
Small piece Work as Large piece EXCEPT increase only to 38 sts and bind off 2 sts 19 times.

MAKING UP

Attach Lacy Pieces as shown in diagram, placing larger piece at right and smaller at left with bind-off tail at ♦. Seam in position. Attach Frills. Sew side seam. Fold waistband to WS along purl ridge and sew loosely, leaving an opening for elastic.
Cut elastic 3" less than waist measurement. Thread elastic through opening, overlap ends by ½", and sew securely. Sew opening closed. Press seams lightly using a damp cloth.

Stitches

 Stockinette

 Seed

— P 1 row on RS

 Attach Lace Edge

Skirt

STANDARD FIT

Skill Intermediate
Fit Standard
Sizes S (M, L)
Approximate measurements
A 37 (42, 46)" after decreases
B 18 (18, 19)" short side, 40" long side, including waistband
Gauge 18 sts and 22 rows to 10cm/4" over St st using smaller needles
Yarn Medium weight
900 (1000, 1100) yds linen blend
Needles 5mm/US8 and 9mm/US13, or size to obtain gauge
Extras 1 yd 1"-wide elastic

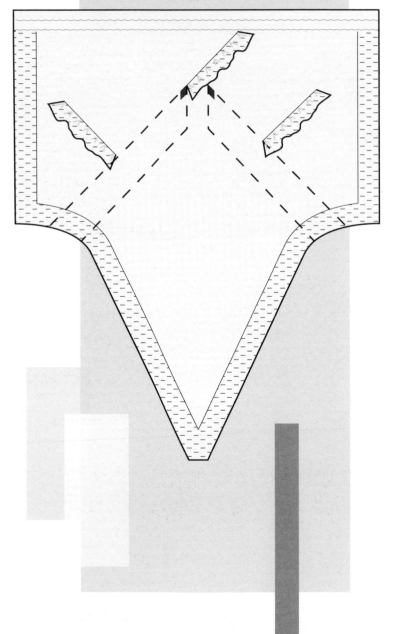

MAGGI'S LINEN in Natural: 8 (9, 9) *balls (for skirt),* 5 (6, 6) *balls (for top)*

KILKENNY TOP, SKIRT, HAT & SCARF

NOTES

1 See *It's Easy,* page 1, for Tassels.
2 Work Top, Scarf, and Hat with 2 strands of linen held together.

Top
SLEEVES

With larger needles, cast on 20 sts.
Work 1 row Seed st.
Next 18 (18, 19)" Work Lacy st.
Work 1 row Seed st.
Bind off very loosely.

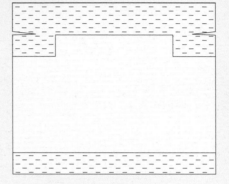

Top

C

B | A

VERY CLOSE FIT

Skill Intermediate

Fit Very close

Sizes S (M, L)

Approximate measurements

A 32 (34½, 37)"

B 13½ (14, 15½)" above hem

C 18 (18, 19)"

Yarn Medium weight
560 (650, 700) yds linen blend

Gauge 13 sts and 17 rows to 10cm/4"
over Seed st with 2 strands of linen
using smaller needles; 12 sts and rows to
12.5cm/5" over Lacy st with 2 strands of
linen using larger needles

Needles 6.5mm/US10½ and 9mm/US13,
or sizes to obtain gauges

Extras Markers, 1½ (2, 2) yds 1"-wide
elastic, matching sewing thread

Hat & Scarf

Skill Easy

Fit Standard

Size One size

Approximate measurements 25" around
(hat), 42" × 20" (triangle scarf)

Gauge 12 sts and rows to 12.5cm/5" over
Lacy stitch with 2 strands of linen

Yarn Medium weight

L 250 yds linen blend (for either)

Needles 9mm/US13, or size to obtain gauge

FRONT AND BACK

With smaller needles, cast on 52
(56, 60) sts.
Work Seed st for 2".
Next 9 (9½, 10)" Work St st.
Next 1½" Work 12 sts Seed st, 28
(32, 36) sts St st, 12 sts Seed st.
Shape underarm, next 2 rows
Bind off 5 (6, 7) sts at beginning
of row, work remaining sts in pat-
tern—42 (44, 46) sts.
**Shape off-shoulder piece, next 2
rows** Cable cast on 8 (10, 12) sts at
beginning of row, work Seed st on
all sts—58 (64, 70) sts.
Next 3 (3, 4)" Work Seed st.
Bind off loosely.

MAKING UP

Sew sleeve and side seams. Sew
seams of off-shoulder piece. Sew
top of Sleeve to underarms for 2"
at side seam. Turn Seed st cuff of
Front and Back to RS and slip st
together every few inches to hold
in place. If desired, weave double
sewing elastic inside top and
bottom of Seed st at off-shoulder
piece to fit tighter.
Press lightly using a damp cloth.

HAT

Cast on 42 sts. Work 6" Seed st.
Work 3" Lacy st.
Next 2 rows Bind off 2 sts, work
Lacy st to end—38 sts.
Next row P1, [k3tog] to last st,
p1—14 sts.
Next row P1, [p3tog] to last st,
p1—6 sts.
Bind off.

MAKING UP

Sew side seam. Roll Seed-st hem
to RS and stitch down. Press
to rounded shape using a damp
cloth. Roll to required length
when wearing.

SCARF

Cast on 6 sts.
Work 2 rows Lacy st.
* Continue in Lacy st, cast on
2 sts at beginning of next 2 rows.
Work 1 row even. Repeat from *
11 times—54 sts.
Cast on 6 sts at beginning of next
8 rows —102 sts.
Work 8 rows even.
Bind off loosely.
Attach a tassel to each end of
bind-off.

*Hat or scarf 2 balls MAGGI'S LINEN
in Natural*

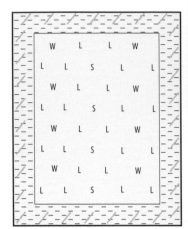

STOCKINETTE STITCH

(St st)
RS rows Knit.
WS rows Purl.

SEED STITCH

Row 1 (RS) * K1, p1; repeat from *.
Row 2 P the knit sts and k the purl sts.
Repeat Row 2 for Seed st.

NOTES

1 See *Techniques,* page 170, for tassels. *2* End each pattern-stitch section with a wrong-side (WS) row.

FRONT AND BACK

With L, cast on 61 sts.
Work Seed st for 1".
Begin borders Keeping 8 sts at beginning and end of every row in Seed st (place markers), work 45 center sts in patterns as follows:
Next 6 rows Work St st.
* **Tassel Row 1** (RS) [P1, k10] 4 times, p1.
Next 2" Work St st.
Tassel Row 2 (RS) K6, [p1, k10] 3 times, p1, k5. **
Next 2" Work St st.
Repeat from * 3 more times, ending last repeat at **.
Next 6 rows Work St st.
Next 1" Work Seed st.
Bind off loosely.

ATTACHING TASSELS

Cushion Back Cut 24" length of L. Fold in half (12"), then in half again (6"). Working on RS of cushion Back, and using crochet hook, attach a tassel in purl st on Tassel Row. Repeat for each purl st in Tassel Rows. Trim tassel ends even.
Cushion Front Cut 48" length of W. Fold in half 3 times and attach in purl sts marked W.
Cut 24" length of S. Fold in half twice and attach in purl sts marked S.
Cut 24" length of L fold in half twice and attach in purl sts marked L.

MAKING UP

Sew edges of pillow together, leaving an opening. Press lightly using a damp cloth. Insert cushion and stitch closed.
Using 2 strands S, whip stitch around edges, making stitches approximately 1" long and 1" apart.

Yarns

	L natural linen
	W white linen
	S silver

Stitches

	Stockinette
	Seed
	Whip

Skill Intermediate
Approximate measurements
14" × 18"
Gauge 18 sts and 24 rows to 10cm/4" over Seed st with L
Yarn Medium weight
L 780 yds linen blend
W 125 yds linen blend
S 85 yds metallic
Needles 5mm/US8, or size to obtain gauge
Extras Markers, crochet hook, 15" × 18" cushion insert

7 balls MAGGI'S LINEN in Natural (L);
1 ball each: MAGGI'S LINEN in White (W)
and MAGGI'S METALLIC in Silver (S)

CASHEL CUSHION

STOCKINETTE STITCH
(St st)
RS rows Knit.
WS rows Purl.

SEED STITCH
Row 1 (RS) * K1, p1; repeat from *.
Row 2 P the knit sts and k the purl sts.
Repeat Row 2 for Seed st.

NOTES
1 See *Techniques*, page 170, for tassels. *2* End each pattern-stitch section with a wrong-side (WS) row.

CUSHION
With L, cast on 100 sts.
Work Seed st for 1".
Decrease row (RS) * K2tog; repeat from * across row—50 sts.
Next row Purl.
Next 2" With M, work Seed st.
* Next 2 rows With L, work St st.
Next 2½" With M, work 8 sts Seed st, 34 sts St st, 8 sts Seed st. Repeat from * until there are 16 L stripes, ending last repeat with 2" Seed st.
Bind off loosely.

FRILL
With L, cast on 110 sts.
Work Seed st for 1".
Decrease row * K2tog; repeat from *—55 sts.
Bind off.

MAKING UP
Sew Frill to 2nd L stripe. With 10 strands of L, weave across row above first L stripe and again below 3rd L stripe, leaving 1" ends. Fold cushion at triangles (shown on illustration at right) with frill edge overlapping bound-off edge. Press lightly using a damp cloth. Insert cushion and seam sides.
Large tassel Cut twelve 18" strands L. Fold in half. With large crochet hook, attach tassel in mohair above frill edge. Trim ends.

6 balls MAGGI'S MOHAIR (M) in Ivory,
2 balls MAGGI'S LINEN (L) in Natural

Yarns

☐ **L** natural linen

☐ **M** ivory mohair

Stitches

☐ Stockinette

▦ Seed

Skill Easy
Approximate measurements
12" × 20"
Gauge 18 sts and 22 rows to 10cm/4" over St st with M
Yarn Medium weight
M 580 yds mohair
L 130 yds linen blend
Needles 5.5mm/US9, or size to obtain gauge
Extras 12" × 20" cushion insert, large crochet hook

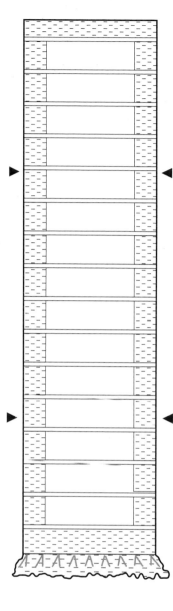

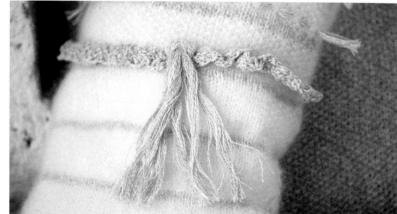

O'BRIEN TABLEMAT

Yarns

- ☐ **L** natural linen
- ☐ **R** white ribbon
- ☐ **W** white linen
- ☐ **S** silver metallic
- ✄ **RY** white rag yarn

Stitches

- ☐ Stockinette
- ⊟ Seed
- 〰 SRS
- ▭ Tube
- ◊ Split

Skill Intermediate
Approximate measurements 12" × 16"
Gauge 18 sts and 24 rows to 10cm/4" over Seed st with L
Yarn Medium weight
For 6 mats
L 1000 yds linen blend
R 90 yds ribbon
W 120 yds linen blend
S 80 yds metallic
RY 65 yds rag yarn
Needles 5mm/US8, or size to obtain gauge
Extras Markers, crochet hook, sewing thread

For 6 mats 8 balls MAGGI'S LINEN (L) in Natural; 1 ball each: MAGGI'S RIBBON (R) in White, MAGGI'S LINEN in White (W), MAGGI'S METALLIC in Silver (S), and MAGGI'S RAG (RY) in White

STOCKINETTE STITCH (St st)
RS rows Knit.
WS rows Purl.

SEED STITCH
Row 1 (RS) * K1, p1; repeat from *.
Row 2 P the knit sts and k the purl sts.
Repeat Row 2 for Seed st.

SINGLE RIDGE STITCH (SRS)
Rows 1 and 3 (RS) Knit.
Rows 2 and 4 (WS) Purl.
Rows 5 and 6 Purl.
Rows 7 and 9 Knit.
Row 8 Purl.
Row 10 Knit.
Repeat Rows 1–10.

TUBE
Beginning with a RS row, work 7 rows St st. (See page 1.)
Close Tube Turn work (WS facing): * Slip 1 st from left-hand (LH) needle to right-hand (RH) needle; insert RH needle under strand running between first st and second st in first row of Tube; slip st on RH needle over strand; continue from * across Tube sts. At end of row, slip last st on LH needle to RH needle.

NOTES
1 See *It's Easy,* page 1, for Splits and Tubes and *Techniques,* page 170, for tassels. *2* End each pattern-stitch section with a wrong-side (WS) row, unless directed to end with a right-side (RS) row. *3* When changing colors, bring new color under old color to prevent holes and work first row in St st. *4* Cut rag yarn (RY) into 8" lengths and knot together, leaving 1" tails (see page 1).

TABLEMAT
With L, cast on 60 sts. Work 1½" Seed st.
Begin borders Keeping 10 sts at beginning and end of every row in Seed st with L (place markers), work center 40 sts in patterns and yarns as follows (unless told to work ALL STS):
Next row (RS) With S, k20; with RY, p20, keeping knots to RS.
Next row With L, k20; with S, p20.
Next 4 rows With L, work St st.
All sts, next 4 rows Work Seed st.

1½" Seed-st Splits (RS) With L, work 10 sts Seed st, turn, work back and forth in Seed st for 1½", ending with a RS row (10-st section); with R, work 10-st section Seed st; work 10-st sections of Seed st in L, R, L, and L.

All sts, next 5 rows With L, work Seed st, except purl across R sts on first (WS) row.

All sts, next 2 rows With S, work as follows: 10 sts Seed st, 40 sts St st, 10 sts Seed st.

* Next row (RS) With L, work 20 sts St st, 20 sts SRS. Work pattern for 9 rows more.

Next row (RS) With L, k5; with W, work 10-st Tube; with L, k15 (Tube sts and next 5 sts), work 20 sts SRS.

Next 9 rows With L, continue SRS and St st as established. *

All sts, next 4 rows Work Seed st.

Repeat from * to *, but reverse placement of SRS and St st/Tube.

All sts, next 2 rows With S, work as follows: 10 sts Seed st, 40 sts St st, 10 sts Seed st.

All sts, next row (RS) With L, work 10 sts Seed st, k40, work 10 sts Seed st.

All sts, next 3 rows Work Seed st.

Next 1½" Repeat Seed-st Splits, working 10-st sections in L, L, R, L, R, then L.

All sts, next 5 rows With L, work Seed st, except purl across R sts on first (WS) row.

Next 2 rows With L, work St st.

Next row (RS) With RY, p20, keeping knots to RS; with S, k20.

Next row With S, p20; with L, k20.

All sts, next 1½" With L, work Seed st except knit across S sts on first (RS) row.
Bind off loosely.

ATTACHING TASSELS

Cut 5" lengths for each tassel: 4 strands of L and 2 strands of S. Fold lengths in half. With crochet hook attach tassel to each corner and 6 more, evenly spaced, along each short side of mat.

MAKING UP

Secure Splits (see page 1). Secure ribbon ends with matching thread. Press lightly using a damp cloth.

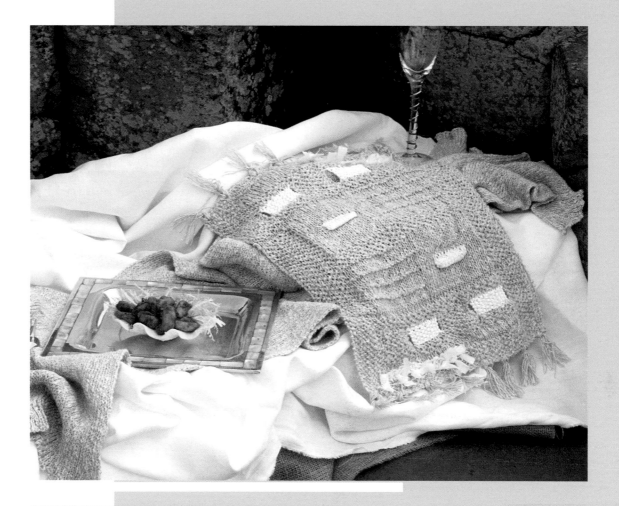

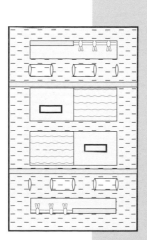

SECTION 2 BLUES

BLUE

Yarns

 T denim tweed

L navy linen

Stitches

☐ Stockinette

▦ Seed

〰 SRS

⬚ AB Rib

▥ P5, K1 Rib

▤ Basket Weave

▭ Tube

◊ Split

OVERSIZED FIT

Skill Intermediate

Fit Loose (man)
  Oversized (woman)

Size S (M, L, 1X)

Approximate measurements

A 45 (48, 51, 54)"

B 28 (29, 29, 29)" plus 3" flap

C 29 (29½, 30, 30)

Gauge Over Seed st: 18 sts and 28 rows to 10cm/4" with L using smaller needles; 15 sts and 24 rows to 10cm/4"with T using larger needles

Yarn

T 960 (960, 1080, 1080) yds wool tweed (Bulky weight)

L 370 yds linen blend (Medium weight)

Needles 5.5mm/US9 and 6mm/US10, or sizes to obtain gauge

Extras Markers

STOCKINETTE STITCH
(St st)
RS rows Knit.
WS rows Purl.

SEED STITCH
Row 1 * K1, p1; repeat from *.
Row 2 P the knit sts and k the purl sts.
Repeat Row 2 for Seed st.

SINGLE RIDGE STITCH
(SRS)
Rows 1 and 3 (RS) Knit.
Rows 2 and 4 (WS) Purl.
Rows 5 and 6 Purl.
Rows 7 and 9 Knit.
Row 8 Purl.
Row 10 Knit.
Repeat Rows 1–10.

ALTERNATING BOBBLE RIB (AB Rib)
Row 1 (RS) * P5, k1; repeat from *.
Rows 2–4 K the knit sts and p the purl sts.
Row 5 P5, * work Bobble [(p1, k1, p1, k1) in next st, turn, k4, turn, p4], p5, k1, p5; repeat from *.
Row 6 K the knit sts and p the purl sts, EXCEPT p the 4 Bobble sts together.
Rows 7–10 Repeat Rows 1–4.
Row 11 P5, k1, p5, * work Bobble in next st, p5, k1, p5, repeat from *.
Row 12 Repeat Row 6.
Repeat Rows 1–12.

P5, K1 RIB
RS rows * P5, k1; repeat from *.
WS rows K the knit sts and p the purl sts.

BASKET WEAVE
Row 1 (RS) * K4, p4; repeat from *.
Rows 2–4 K the knit sts and p the purl sts.
Row 5 * P4, k4; repeat from *.
Rows 6–8 K the knit sts and p the purl sts.
Repeat Rows 1–8.

TUBE
Beginning with a RS row, work 7 rows in St st.
Close Tube Turn work (WS facing): * Slip 1 st from left-hand (LH) needle to right-hand (RH) needle; insert RH needle under strand running between first st and second st on first row of Tube; slip st on RH needle over strand; continue from * across Tube sts. At end of row, slip last st on LH needle to RH needle.

NOTES
1 See *It's Easy*, page 1, for Splits and Tubes **2** Use 2 strands of L held together EXCEPT for Hem Extensions. **3** End each pattern-stitch section with a wrong-side (WS) row, unless directed to end with a right-side (RS) row. **4** When changing colors, always work first row in St st.

RIGHT SLEEVE
With T, cast on 36 (38, 40, 42) sts. Work Seed st for 3".
Begin increasing Increase 1 st at beginning and end of every RS row (except Tube rows) to 60 sts, then every other RS row to top of sleeve; AT SAME TIME, work patterns and yarns as follows: Work Basket Weave for 3". *
Work St st 2 rows L and 2" T.
**** 2" Seed-st Splits** Mark center 10 sts. With T, work Seed st to center sts, turn, work back and forth on edge sts for 2", ending with a RS row (Seed-st section); with L, work Seed-st section on center 10 sts; with T, work Seed-st edge section on remaining sts.
Next row (WS) With T, p across all sts. **
Next 3" Work St st.
Tube (RS) With L, work Tube on all sts.
< Next 3 (3, 3, 2)" With T, work Seed st to center 35 sts, work 35 sts in AB Rib, work Seed st to end.
Next 1" Work Seed st.
Bind off loosely.

LEFT SLEEVE
Work as Right Sleeve to *. With L, work 2 rows St st. Work as Right Sleeve from ** to **.
> Work St st for 1½".
Next row (RS) With T, knit to 14 center sts. With L, work Tube over 14 sts. With T, k these 14 sts and to end of row.
Repeat from > once more.
Next 2" With T, work St st for 1½". With L, work 2 rows St st. Work as Right Sleeve from < to end.

BACK AND FRONT
With T, cast on 84 (90, 96, 102) sts. Work Seed st for 3".
Next row (RS) With L, work 36 (40, 44, 48)-st Tube; with T, k

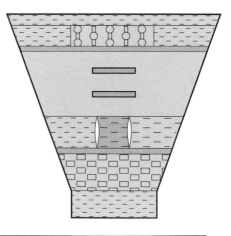

8 (8, 9, 9) balls MAGGI'S TWEED FLECK CHUNKY (T) in Denim; 3 balls MAGGI'S LINEN (L) in Navy

Tube sts and work Basket Weave to end.

Next 4" With T, work Basket Weave.

Next row (RS) With T, k to last 36 (40, 44, 48) sts; with L, work Tube over 36 (40, 44, 48) sts; with T, k Tube sts.

Next 3" With T, work Seed st.

Next 2 rows With L, work St st.

2" Seed-st Splits With T, work 12 (15, 18, 21)-st Seed-st section, ending with a RS row; work 10-st sections in: T, L, L, T, L, T; with L, work last section over remaining sts.

Next row (WS) With T, purl.

Next 2 rows With L, work St st.

Next row With T, work SRS over first 48 (51, 55, 58) sts and work remaining 36 (39, 41, 44) sts in AB Rib. Work patterns for 6".

* **Next row** (RS) With L, k to center 50 sts, work 50-st Tube, k Tube sts and to end of row.

Next row (WS) Purl. *

Next row With T, work 48 (51, 55, 58) sts in P5, K1 Rib; work 36 (39, 41, 44) sts SRS. Work patterns for 4".

Repeat from * to *.

Next 3 (4, 4, 4)" With T, work Basket Weave.

Work St st 2 rows L, 2 rows T, and 2 rows L.

Next 3" With T, work Seed st. (Adjust length here if desired, but work no less than 1" of Seed st.) Bind off loosely.

HEM EXTENSIONS (make 2)
With smaller needles and single strand of L, cast on 96 (112, 118, 124) sts. Work Seed st for 7". Bind off.

MAKING UP
Secure Splits (see page 1). Sew shoulder seams, leaving approximately 12" open at center. Sew Sleeves to body, centering Sleeve at shoulder seam. Sew side seams, leaving bottom 3" open. Sew Sleeve seams. Sew Hem Extension to inside of sweater Front and Back 4" above bottom edge, leaving sides open. Press lightly using a damp cloth.

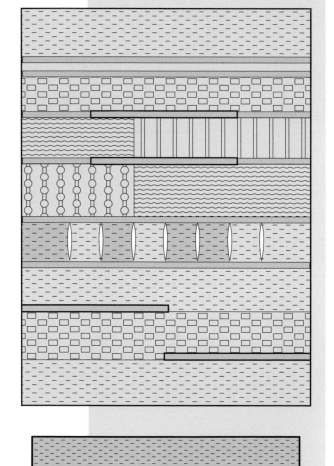

Thatched roofs, canopied beds, fancy mantles, stepped chimneys, an enameled tub—all the modern conveniences.

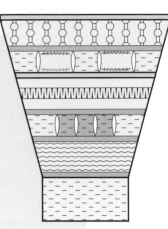

Yarns

L natural linen

R navy ribbon

M navy linen

Stitches

Stockinette

Seed

SRS

AB Rib

P5, K1 Rib

Ladder

Tube

Split

Ruffle

LOOSE FIT

Skill Intermediate

Fit Loose

Size S (M, L)

Approximate measurements

A 43 (47, 51)"

B Front 39" long, Back 41"

C 27½ (28½, 28½)"

Gauge 18 sts and 22 rows to 10cm/4"
over St st with L

Yarn Medium weight

L 1560 (1660, 1740) yds linen blend

R 195 yds ribbon

M 85 yds linen

Needles 5mm/US8, or size to obtain gauge

Extras Markers, three ¾" buttons, sewing
thread and needle

STOCKINETTE STITCH
(St st)

RS rows Knit.

WS rows Purl.

SEED STITCH

Row 1 (RS) * K1, p1; repeat
from *.

Row 2 P the knit sts and k the
purl sts.

Repeat Row 2 for Seed st.

SINGLE RIDGE STITCH
(SRS)

Rows 1 and 3 (RS) Knit.

Rows 2 and 4 (WS) Purl.

Rows 5 and 6 Purl.

Rows 7 and 9 Knit.

Row 8 Purl.

Row 10 Knit.

Repeat Rows 1–10.

ALTERNATING BOBBLE
RIB (AB Rib)

Row 1 (RS) * P5, k1; repeat
from *.

Rows 2–4 K the knit sts and p the
purl sts.

Row 5 P5, * work Bobble (p1, k1,
p1, k1) in next st, turn, k4, turn,
p4], p5, k1, p5; repeat from *.

Row 6 K the knit sts and p the
purl sts EXCEPT p the 4 Bobble
sts together.

Rows 7–10 Repeat Rows 1–4.

Row 11 P5, k1, p5, * work Bobble
in next st, p5, k1, p5; repeat from *.

Row 12 Repeat Row 6.

Repeat Rows 1–12.

P5, K1 RIB

RS rows * P5, k1; repeat from *.

WS rows K the knit sts and p the
purl sts.

LADDER STITCH

Row 1 (RS) Knit, wrapping yarn
around the needle 2 times for
every stitch (see page 170).

Row 2 Purl into sts, dropping
wrap off needle.

RUFFLE STITCH

Row 1 (RS) Knit.

Row 2 Purl into front and back of
every st.

Rows 3–9 Work in St st.

Row 10 P2 tog across.

Row 11 Knit.

TUBE

Beginning with a RS row, work 7
rows St st.

Close Tube Turn work (WS
facing): * Slip 1 st from left-hand
(LH) needle to right-hand (RH)
needle; insert RH needle under
strand running between first st
and second st in first row of Tube;
slip st on RH needle over strand;
continue from * across Tube sts.
At end of row, slip last st on LH
needle to RH needle.

NOTES

1 See *It's Easy*, page 1, for Tubes
and Splits and *Techniques*, page
170, for cable cast-on. *2* End
each pattern-stitch section with
a wrong-side (WS) row unless
directed to end with a right-side
(RS) row. *3* Work first row of a
new color in St st.

Cardi
SLEEVES

With L, cast on 60 sts. Work Seed
st for 4".

Next 2 rows With R, work St st.

Begin increasing Increase 1 st at
beginning and end of every 3rd row
to top of sleeve, AT SAME TIME,
work patterns and yarns as follows:

Next 3 (3, 2)" With L, work SRS.

Next 2 rows With R, work St st.

2" Seed-st Splits Mark center 30
sts. With L, work Seed st to center
sts, turn, work Seed st back and
forth on edge sts for 2", ending
with a RS row (Seed-st section);
* with R, work a Seed-st section on
next 10 sts; repeat from * 2 times;
with L, work a Seed-st section on
remaining sts.

Work St st 2 rows R, 3 rows L.

Next 2 rows Work Ladder st.

Next 4 rows Work St st.

Tube With M, work Tube over
all sts.

11-row Splits With L, work Seed
st to center 50 sts, turn, work back
and forth for 10 more rows; work
20-st section Ruffle st, 10-st section Seed st, 20-st section Ruffle
st, and Seed-st section on remaining sts.

Next 2 rows With R, work St st,
beginning with a WS row.

Next row (WS) With L, purl.

Next 3" Work AB Rib.

Tube With M, work Tube over
all sts.

With L, bind off loosely.

*Cardi 13 (14, 15) balls MAGGI'S LINEN
(L) in Natural; 2 balls MAGGI'S RIBBON
(R) in Navy; 1 ball Linen (M) in Navy*

RIGHT FRONT

With L, cast on 40 sts. Work Seed st for 3".

At beginning of next WS row, cable cast on 10 (14, 18) sts and continue Seed st on 50 (54, 58) sts for 2".

Begin border Keeping 8 sts at beginning and end of every row in Seed st with L (place markers), work patterns and yarns on center sts as follows (unless told to work ALL STS):

Next 3 (4, 4)" Work SRS.

Next 3" [Work 2 rows Ladder st on all sts. Work center sts St st for 1"] 2 times.

All sts, work St st 2 rows R, 2 rows L, 2 rows R, 1 row L.

Next 4 (5, 5)" Work P5, K1 Rib.

* All sts With L, work Seed st for 2", 2 rows Ladder st, St st for 1", 2 rows Ladder st.

End side border Keeping 8 sts at center front in Seed st with L, work on remaining 42 (46, 50) sts as follows:

< Next 3" Work SRS.

Shape neck Decrease 1 st at center front every 6th row on RS (by working Seed st border, then k2tog) 8 (10, 12) times—42 (44, 46) sts. AT SAME TIME, work patterns and yarns as follows:

** All sts, next 1" With R, work Seed st border and St st.

All sts, next row (RS) With L, knit.

Next 4" Beginning with Row 2, work AB Rib.

All sts, next 2 rows With R, work St st.

Next 1½" With L, work St st.

<< Next row Knit to center 14 sts of remaining sts; with M, work 14-st Tube; with L, k to end .

Next 1" With L, work St st. Repeat from <<, working St st for 3" instead of 1".

All sts, next 2 rows Work Ladder st.

All sts, next 2 rows With R, work St st.

All sts, next 2" With L, work Seed st. Adjust length here if required. Bind off loosely.

LEFT FRONT

Work as Right Front, reversing shaping and pattern placement.

BACK

Begin as two separate pieces, then join.

Right Side

With L, cast on 44 sts. Work Seed st for 5".

Cable cast on 10 (14, 18) sts at beginning of next (RS) row and continue Seed st on 54 (58, 62) sts for 2".

Work as Fronts from Begin border to *; leave sts on a spare needle.

Left Side

Work as Right Side but cast on additional sts at beginning of WS row.

Join pieces (RS) Work Seed st across Right Side to last 8 sts, then with needle holding these 8 sts held in front of needle holding Left Side sts, * work first st from each needle together (k2tog or p2tog to maintain Seed st); repeat from * across 8 sts of Right Side; work Seed st across remaining sts of Left Side—100 (108, 116) sts.

Next 2" Continue Seed st.

Next 2" Work 2 rows Ladder st, St st for 1", 2 rows Ladder st. Keeping center 16 sts Seed st, work to match Fronts from < to shoulder bind-off. EXCEPT do not shape neck.

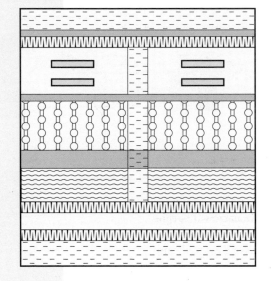

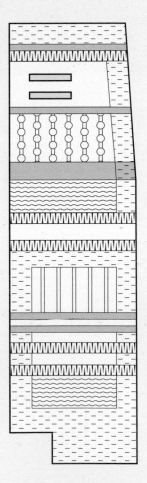

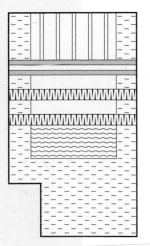

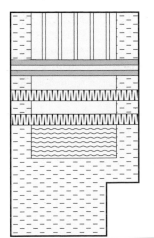

COLLAR

With L, cast on 10 sts. Work Seed st for 4". Continuing Seed st, work increases and decreases on right edge of collar (at beginning of RS rows and end of WS rows) to shape collar as follows: Increase 1 st every row 30 times—40 sts; work 1" even; decrease every 3rd row 28 times—12 sts; work 12" even; increase every 3rd row 20 times—32 sts; work 1" even; decrease every row 22 times—10 sts; work 4" even. Bind off.

EPAULETTES (make 2)

With L, cast on 10 sts. Work Seed st for 6". Bind off.

MAKING UP

Secure Splits (see page 1). Sew shoulder seams. Centering Sleeves at shoulders, sew Sleeves to body. Sew sides above narrow R stripes. Sew sleeve seams. Pin center of Collar to center of Back neck and sew to neck edge. Press seams. Sew button through both layers of center Back 2" below join. Sew one end of each Epaulette at neck edge on shoulder seam and sew button through Epaulette and shoulder seam 1½" from other end.

Shoulder pads are recommended to be worn with this garment.

BALLINADEE CARDI & WAISTCOAT

Yarns

L natural linen

N navy linen

R navy ribbon

 RY denim rag yarn

Stitches

Stockinette

Seed

SRS

P4, K2 Rib

Tube

Split

LOOSE FIT

Skill Intermediate

Fit Loose

Size S (M, L)

Approximate measurements

A 38 (42, 46)"

B 14–15" to point at front

Gauge 18 sts and 22 rows to 10cm/4" over Seed st with L

Yarn Medium weight

L 500 (630, 750) yds linen blend

N 120 yds linen blend

R 95 yds ribbon

RY 65 yds rag yarn

Needles 5 mm/US8, or size to obtain gauge

Extras Markers, five ¾" buttons, sewing thread and needle

STOCKINETTE STITCH

(St st)

RS rows Knit.

WS rows Purl.

SEED STITCH

Row 1 (RS) * K1, p1; repeat from *.

Row 2 P the knit sts and k the purl sts.

Repeat Row 2 for Seed st.

SINGLE RIDGE STITCH (SRS)

Rows 1 and 3 (RS) Knit.

Rows 2 and 4 (WS) Purl.

Rows 5 and 6 Purl.

Rows 7 and 9 Knit.

Row 8 Purl.

Row 10 Knit.

Repeat Rows 1–10.

P4, K2 RIB

RS rows * P4, k2; repeat from *.

WS rows K the knit sts and p the purl sts.

TUBE

Beginning with a RS row, work 7 rows St st. (See page 1.)

Close Tube Turn work (WS facing): * Slip 1 st from left-hand (LH) needle to right-hand (RH) needle; insert RH needle under strand running between first st and second st on first row of Tube; slip st on RH needle over strand; continue from * across Tube sts. At end of row, slip last st on LH needle to RH needle.

NOTES

1 See *Techniques*, page 170, for cable cast-on and ssk. *2* End each pattern-stitch section with a wrong-side (WS) row, unless directed to end with a right-side (RS) row. *3* When changing colors, bring new color under old color to prevent

holes and work first row in St st. *4* Cut rag yarn into 8" lengths and knot together, leaving 1" tails.

Waistcoat

LEFT FRONT

With L, cast on 14 sts. Work 1½" in Seed st. Cable cast on 14 sts at beginning of next RS row and continue Seed st on 28 sts for 1½". Cast on 14 (16, 20) sts at beginning of next RS row and continue Seed st on 42 (44, 48) sts for 1½". Cast on 8 (10, 10) sts at beginning of next WS row and continue Seed st on 50 (54, 58) sts for 1 (2, 2)".

Next row (RS) With N, work Tube over 42 (46, 50) sts; with L, k to last 8 sts; work 8 sts Seed st.

Begin border Keeping 8 sts at center front (at end of RS rows and beginning of WS rows) in Seed st with L (place markers), work remaining sts in patterns and yarns as follows (unless told to work ALL STS):

Next row (WS) With L, purl.

Next 4" Work SRS.

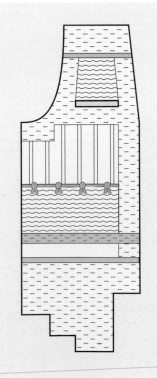

RIGHT FRONT

Work as Left Front (EXCEPT cast on sts at beginning of WS row twice and RS row once) until 50 (54, 58) sts on needle.

Next 1 (2, 2)" Work even in Seed st, AT SAME TIME, on RS row, work a buttonhole to match bottom button marker on Left Front (work 3 sts Seed st, yarn over, k2tog, work 3 sts Seed st, work pattern to end).

Begin border Keeping 8 sts at center front (at beginning of RS rows and end of WS rows) in Seed st with L, work remaining sts in patterns and yarns as follows (unless told to work ALL STS), working buttonholes to match Left Front markers:

All sts, next 2 rows With R, work St st.

All sts, next 6 rows With R, work Seed st.

Next row (RS) With L, knit.

Next 4" Work P4, K2 Rib (begin on WS row: k4, p2).

Next row (RS) With L, k12; with RY, purl, keeping knots to RS.

Next row (WS) With L, k RY sts, p12.

Next 3" Work Seed st.

Begin armhole and neck shaping:

Next row (RS) Bind off 10 (14, 14) sts, work Seed st to end.

Next row Work Seed st.

Next row (RS) With R, k6, ssk, k to last 2 sts before border, k2tog, k8.

Next row Purl.

Add armhole border Keeping 6 sts at armhole (at beginning of RS rows and end of WS rows) in Seed st with L, work decreases on center sts as follows: ssk at armhole once, and k2tog at neck edge every 4th row until 26 (28, 30) sts; AT SAME TIME, work patterns and yarns on center sts as follows: with L, work SRS for 4"; with N,

work Tube; with L, work Seed st until armhole measures 7 (7, 8)". Bind off loosely.

Mark center front edge for 5 buttons, one 1" above last cast-on, another at the beginning of neck shaping, and 3 spaced evenly between.

Next 1" With L, work St st.

All sts, next 1" With R, work Seed st.

Next 4" With L, work SRS.

Next row (RS) With RY, p to end, keeping knots to RS.

Next row With L, knit.

Next 4" Work P4, K2 Rib.

Next row (RS) Continue Rib to last 14 sts, work 14 sts Seed st. Work pattern for 2", ending with RS row.

Begin armhole and neck shaping:

Next row (WS) Bind off 10 (14, 14) sts, work Seed st to end.

Next row Ssk, work Seed st to last 8 sts, k2tog, work Seed st to end.

Next row Work Seed st.

Add armhole border Keeping 6 sts at armhole (at end of RS rows and beginning of WS rows) in

Seed st with L, work decreases on center sts as follows: k2tog at armhole once, and ssk at neck edge every 4th row until 26 (28, 30) sts remain. AT SAME TIME, work patterns and yarns on center sts as follows: with N, work Tube; with L, work SRS for 4"; with R, work 2 rows St st across all sts; with L, work Seed st until armhole matches Left Front.
Bind off loosely.

BACK
With L, cast on 88 (92, 96) sts.
Work Seed st for 2".
Work SRS until Back measures 11".
Next 1" Work 14 sts at beginning and end of rows Seed st and continue SRS on center 60 (64, 68) sts.
Begin armhole shaping: Keeping center sts in SRS and edges in Seed st, bind off 8 sts at beginning of next 2 rows—72 (76, 80) sts.
Next 2 RS rows Work 6 sts Seed st, ssk, work SRS to last 8 sts, k2tog, work 6 sts Seed st. Work pattern on 68 (72, 76) sts until armhole measures 5 (5, 6)".
Work all sts Seed st until same length as Front armhole.
Bind off 26 (28, 30) sts at beginning of next 2 rows.
Bind off remaining sts.

OPTIONAL WAIST TAB
With N, cast on 10 sts. Work Seed st for 3". Bind off.

MAKING UP
Secure ribbon ends with matching thread. Sew shoulder and side seams.
Optional: At center Back, 3" above bottom, gather center 5" with sewing thread. Place Tab over gathers and sew ends to Back. Press seams and Front edges lightly using a damp cloth. Sew buttons to Left Front.

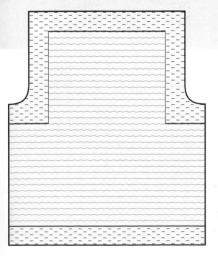

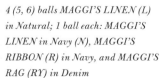

4 (5, 6) balls MAGGI'S LINEN (L) in Natural; 1 ball each: MAGGI'S LINEN in Navy (N), MAGGI'S RIBBON (R) in Navy, and MAGGI'S RAG (RY) in Denim

Yarns

- ▢ **L** natural linen
- ▨ **D** denim
- ▢ **R** ivory ribbon

Stitches

- ▢ Stockinette
- ▦ Seed
- ▤ SRS
- ⬡ AB Rib
- ▥ K5, P5 Rib
- ▭ Tube
- ⬦ Split

Skill Intermediate

One size

Approximate measurements

A 25" wide

B 62" long

Gauge 18 sts and 24 rows to 10cm/4" over Seed st

Yarn Medium weight

L 1000 yds linen blend

D 110 yds denim

R 95 yds ribbon

Needles 5.5mm/US9, or size to obtain gauge

Extras Markers, stitch holder, sewing thread

STOCKINETTE STITCH
(St st)
RS rows Knit.
WS rows Purl.

SEED STITCH
Row 1 (RS) * K1, p1; repeat from *.
Row 2 P the knit sts and k the purl sts.
Repeat Row 2 for Seed st.

SINGLE RIDGE STITCH
(SRS)
Rows 1 and 3 (RS) Knit.
Rows 2 and 4 (WS) Purl.
Rows 5 and 6 Purl.
Rows 7 and 9 Knit.
Row 8 Purl.
Row 10 Knit.
Repeat Rows 1–10.

ALTERNATING BOBBLE
RIB (AB Rib)
Row 1 (RS) * P5, k1; repeat from *.
Rows 2–4 K the knit sts and p the purl sts.
Row 5 P5; * work Bobble [(p1, k1, p1, k1) in next st, turn, k4, turn, p4], p5, k1, p5; repeat from *.
Row 6 K the knit sts and p the purl sts, EXCEPT p the 4 Bobble sts together.
Rows 7–10 Repeat Rows 1–4.
Row 11 P5, k1, p5, * work Bobble in next st, p5, k1, p5; repeat from *.
Row 12 Repeat Row 6.
Repeat Rows 1–12.

K5, P5 RIB
RS rows * K5, p5; repeat from *.
WS rows K the knit sts and p the purl sts.

TUBE
Beginning with a RS row, work 7 rows St st .
Close Tube Turn work (WS facing): * Slip 1 st from left-hand (LH) needle to right-hand (RH) needle; insert RH needle under strand running between first st and second st in first row of Tube; slip st on RH needle over strand; continue from * across Tube sts. At end of row, slip last st on LH needle to RH needle.

NOTES
1 See *It's Easy*, page 1, for Tubes and Splits and *Techniques*, page 170, for cable cast-on. **2** End each pattern-stitch section with a wrong-side (WS) row. **3** Work first row of a new color in St st.

SHAWL
With L, cast on 20 sts. Work Seed st for 1½".
[Cable cast on 15 sts at beginning of next 2 rows and continue Seed st for 1½"] 3 times—110 sts.
Next 2 rows With D, work St st.
Begin Seed-st borders Keeping 10 sts at beginning and end of each row Seed st with L (place markers), work center 90 sts in patterns and yarns as follows to neck opening (unless told to work ALL STS):
Next 2" With L, work St st.
All sts, next 2 rows With D, work St st.
Next row With L, work 45 sts SRS, 45 sts AB Rib. Work pattern for 5".
All sts, next 2 rows With D, work St st.
All sts, 2" Seed-st Splits With L, work 10 sts Seed st, turn, work back and forth on these sts for 2", ending with a RS row (10-st section); with D, work a 10-st section;

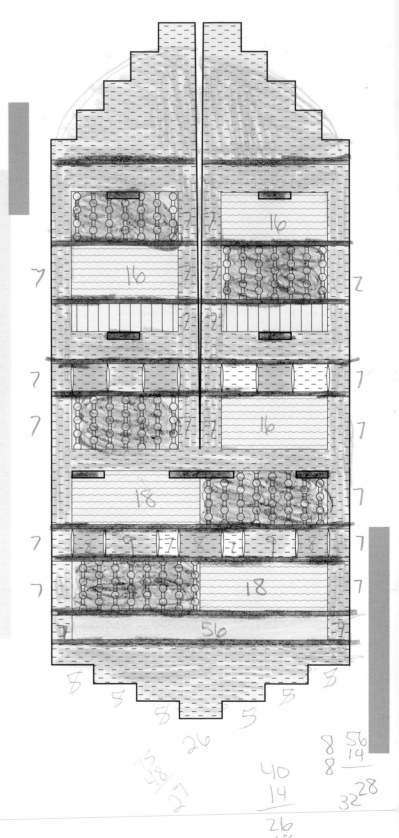

with L, work a 17-st section; with R, work a 10-st section; with D, work a 16-st section; with R, work a 10-st section; with L, work a 17-st section; with D, work a 10-st section; with L, work a 10-st section.

All sts, next 2 rows With D, work St st.

All sts, next row (WS) With L, purl.

Next row Work 45 sts AB Rib, 45 sts SRS. Work pattern for 5".

Tube Row 1 (RS) With D, work Tube over 10 sts; with L, k37 (Tube sts and next 27 sts); with D, work Tube over 16 sts; with L, k43; with D, work Tube over 10 sts; with L, k10.

Next row (WS) With L, purl.

All sts, next 2" Work Seed st.

Divide for neck, all sts, next row (RS) Work 10 sts Seed st (border), 35 sts SRS, 10 sts Seed st (center front border). Turn and work back and forth on these 55 sts, placing remaining 55 sts on a holder. Keeping 10-st Seed-st borders at beginning and end of each row, work center 35 sts as follows:

Next 5" Work SRS.

All sts, next 2 rows With D, work St st.

All sts, 2" Seed-st Splits With L, work a 10-st section of Seed st; with R, a 10-st section; with D, a 15-st section; with R, a 10-st section; with L, a 10-st section.

All sts, next 2 rows With D, work St st.

All sts, next row (WS) With L, purl.

Next 2" Work Seed st.

Tube Row 2 (RS) With L, work 12 sts Seed st; with D, work Tube over 12 sts; with L, k12 (Tube sts) and work 11 sts Seed st.

Next 3" With L, work K5, P5 Rib (begin on WS: p5, k5).

* All sts, next row (RS) With D, purl.

All sts, next row (WS) With L, knit. *****

Next 5" Work AB Rib. Repeat from * to *.

Next 5" Work SRS.

Next row (RS) Repeat Tube Row 2.

End borders Work over all sts as follows:

Next 3" With L, work Seed st.

Next 2 rows With D, work St st.

Next 1" With L, work Seed st.

[**Next row** (RS) Bind off 10 sts, work Seed st to end. **Next 3"** Work Seed st] 4 times—15 sts. Bind off remaining sts.

Left side Repeat patterns and yarns with 55 sts from holder, EXCEPT reverse placement of SRS and AB Rib and work Splits in D and L, as shown on chart, and at end, bind off at beginning of WS rows instead of RS rows.

MAKING UP

Secure Splits (see page 1). Secure ribbon ends with matching thread. Press lightly using a damp cloth.

8 balls MAGGI'S LINEN (L) in Natural;
2 balls MAGGI'S DENIM (D) in Mid Blue;
1 ball MAGGI'S RIBBON (R) in Ivory

STOCKINETTE STITCH
(St st)
RS rows Knit.
WS rows Purl.

SEED STITCH
Row 1 (RS) * K1, p1; repeat from *.
Row 2 P the knit sts and k the purl sts.
Repeat Row 2 for Seed st.

TUBE
Beginning with a RS row, work 9 rows St st. (See page 1.)
Close Tube Turn work (WS facing): * Slip 1 st from left-hand (LH) needle to right-hand (RH) needle; insert RH needle under strand running between first st and second st in first row of Tube; slip st on RH needle over strand; continue from * across Tube sts. At end of row, slip last st on LH needle to RH needle.

NOTE
End each pattern stitch section with a wrong-side (WS) row, unless told to end with a RS row.

Yarns

T denim or cerise tweed

M ivory or denim mohair

R red rag or mustard linen

Stitches

Stockinette

Seed

Tube

LOOSE FIT

Skill Intermediate
Fit Loose
Size 4 (6, 8, 10)
Approximate measurements
A 29 (31½, 32½, 35)", buttoned
B 14 (14, 16, 16)"
C 19 (20, 21, 22)"
Gauge 14 sts and 22 rows to 10cm/4" over St st
Yarn Bulky weight
T 270 (360, 480, 480) yds wool tweed Medium weight
M 110 yds mohair or linen blend
R 65 yds rag yarn or mohair
Needles 6mm/US10, or size to obtain gauge
Buttons Four ¾"

Kid's Cardi
BACK
With T, cast on 46 (50, 52, 56) sts.
Work Seed st for 10 rows.
Work 2 rows St st.
* **Next row** (RS) With T, k2 (4, 5, 7); [with R, work 6-st Tube; with T, k12 (Tube sts and next 6 sts)] 3 times; with R, work 6-st Tube; with T, k Tube sts and to end.
Next 5 (5, 7, 7) rows With T, work St st, beginning with a WS row. **
Next row (RS) With T, k8 (10, 11, 13); [with M, work 6-st Tube; with T, k12] 2 times; with M, work 6-st Tube; with T, k to end.
Next 5 (5, 7, 7) rows With T, work St st, beginning with a WS row.
Repeat from * once.
Repeat from * to ** once.
Tube With R, work a Tube across all sts.
Shape armholes With T, work 2 rows St st, binding off 3 sts at the beginning of each row—40 (44, 46, 50) sts.
Change to Seed st, AT SAME TIME, decrease 1 st at beginning and end of next 5 (6, 6, 7) rows—30 (32, 34, 36) sts.
Work even until armholes measure 5½ (6, 6, 6½)".
Bind off 8 (8, 10,10) sts at beginning of next 2 rows.
Bind off remaining sts.

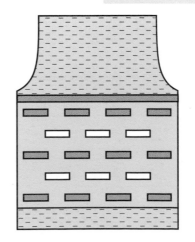

RIGHT FRONT
With T, cast on 23 (25, 26, 28) sts.
Work 10 rows Seed st.
Work 2 rows St st.
* **Next row** (RS) With T, k2 (3, 4, 5); with R, work 6-st Tube; with T, k12; with R, work 6-st Tube; with T, k to end.
Next 5 (5, 7, 7) rows With T, work St st, beginning with a WS row. **
Next row (RS) With T, k8 (9, 10, 11); with M, work 6-st Tube; with T, k to end.
Next 5 (5, 7, 7) rows With T, work St st, beginning with a WS row.
Repeat from * once.
Begin neck shaping Repeat from * to ** once, AT SAME TIME, k2tog at beginning of next RS row and every following 6th row.
Tube With R, work a Tube across all sts.
Shape armhole With T, work 2 rows St st, binding off 3 sts at beginning of WS rows. Change to Seed st, AT SAME TIME, decrease 1 st at armhole next 5 (6, 6, 7) rows. Continue to decrease at front edge only to 8 (8, 10, 10) sts. Work even to match Back.
Bind off.

3 (3, 4, 4) balls MAGGI'S TWEED FLECK CHUNKY in Denim or Cerise (T); 1 ball each: MAGGI'S MOHAIR in Ivory or Denim (M) and MAGGI'S RAG in Red or MAGGI'S LINEN in Mustard (R)

LEFT FRONT

Work as Right Front, reversing shaping.

SLEEVES

With T, cast on 24 (26, 26, 28) sts.
Work 12 rows Seed st.
Work 2 (4, 4, 4) rows St st.
Begin increasing Increase 1 st at beginning and end of 6th row and every following 6 (8, 8, 8)th row to 32 (32, 36, 36) sts, then every 4th row to 34 (36, 38, 40) sts, AT SAME TIME, working in patterns and yarns as follows:
* **Next row** (RS) Mark center 6 sts. With T, k to center sts; with R, work 6-st Tube; with T, k to end.
Next 5 (5, 7, 7) rows With T, work St st, beginning with a WS row. **
Next row (RS) With T, k to center 18 sts; with M, work 6-st Tube; with T, k12; with M, work 6-st Tube; with T, k to end.
Next 5 (5, 7, 7) rows With T, work St st, beginning with a WS row.
Repeat from * once.
Repeat from * to ** once.
(Lengthen here if required.)
Tube With R, work a Tube across all sts.
Begin cap shaping With T, k 1 row then work Seed st AT SAME TIME binding off 1 st at beginning of next 14 (16, 14, 18) rows—20 (20, 24, 22) sts.
Next 2 rows Work even.
Bind off 2 sts at beginning of next 4 (4, 6, 4) rows.
Bind off remaining sts.

FRONT BAND

Sew shoulder seams.
Cast on 12 sts with T and work 4 rows Seed st.
Next (Buttonhole) row (RS) K1, p1, k1, yarn over, k2tog, p1, k1, p1, yarn over, k2tog, k1, p1.
Next 4 (4, 5, 5)" Work Seed st.
Next row (RS) Repeat Buttonhole row.
Work Seed st until Band fits up Right Front, around neck, and down Left Front, slightly stretched.
Bind off.

MAKING UP

Sew Sleeve and side seams. Fit Sleeves into armholes and sew. Sew Band to sweater. Sew buttons on left side of Band to match buttonholes.

HEADBAND

With T, cast on 10 sts. Work 34" Seed st.
Bind off.

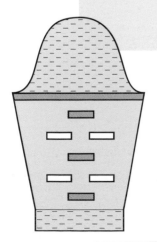

LACY STITCH
EVEN NUMBER OF STS
All rows P1 * yarn over, p2tog; repeat from *,
end p1.

NOTES
1 See *It's Easy*, page 1, for hand-knotting Rag
Mix. *2* When knitting with Rag Mix, keep knots
to right side (RS).

Color sequence for hand-knotting Rag Mix
Cut fifty 10" lengths of each yarn. Cut additional
lengths as needed. Knot strands together in the
following order: L, M, RY, I, D, R, leaving 1"
tails on knots.

TABLEMAT
With Rag Mix, cast on 28 sts.
Work Lacy St for 16".
Bind off loosely.

MAKING UP
Press lightly using a damp cloth.

Skills Intermediate

Approximate measurements
12" × 16"

Gauge 6 sts and 6 rows to 12.5cm/
5" over Lacy St

Yarn Medium weight
for 6 mats, 50 yds each:

L linen blend

M mohair

RY rag yarn

I mohair

D denim

R ribbon

Needles 9mm/US13, or size to
obtain gauge

Extras Sewing thread and needles

For 6 mats 1 ball each: MAGGI'S LINEN
(L) in Natural, MAGGI'S MOHAIR (M)
in Denim, MAGGI'S RAG (RY) in Denim,
MAGGI'S MOHAIR in Ivory (I), MAGGI'S
DENIM (D) in Pale Blue, and MAGGI'S
RIBBON (R) in Ivory

SECTION 3 GREENS

Home to a cottier (a farm hand whose only land was a small potato garden), at Ulster Folk and Transport Museum.

Yarns

L natural linen

O olive linen

S beige/olive slub

R olive rag yarn

Stitches

Stockinette

Seed

SRS

P4, K4 Rib

P5, K1 Rib

Basket Weave

Ladder

Tube

~~~ Purl RS row

vvv Increase

^^^ Decrease

C

B A

LOOSE FIT

Skill Intermediate

Fit Loose

Size S (M, L)

Approximate measurements

A 40 (43, 46)"

B 27 (29, 31)" at sides

C 28 (29, 28½)"

Gauge 18 sts and 22 rows to 10cm/4" over Seed st in L

Yarn Medium weight

L 1325 (1460, 1575) yds linen blend

O 250 yds linen blend

S 85 yds slub

R 65 yds rag yarn

Needles 5mm/US8, or size to obtain gauge

Extras Stitch markers

STOCKINETTE STITCH
(St st)
RS Rows Knit.
WS Rows Purl.

SEED STITCH
Row 1 * K1, p1; repeat from *.
Row 2 P the knit sts and k the purl sts.
Repeat Row 2 for Seed st.

SINGLE RIDGE STITCH
(SRS)
Rows 1 and 3 (RS) Knit.
Rows 2 and 4 (WS) Purl.
Rows 5 and 6 Purl.
Rows 7 and 9 Knit.
Row 8 Purl.
Row 10 Knit.
Repeat Rows 1–10.

P4, K4 RIB
RS Rows * P4, k4; repeat from *.
WS Rows K the knit sts and p the purl sts.

P5, K1 RIB
RS Rows * P5, k1; repeat from *.
WS Rows K the knit sts and p the purl sts.

BASKET WEAVE
Row 1 (RS) * K4, p4; repeat from *.
Rows 2–4 K the knit sts and p the purl sts.
Row 5 * P4, k4; repeat from *.
Rows 6–8 K the knit sts and p the purl sts.
Repeat Rows 1–8.

LADDER STITCH
Row 1 (RS) Knit, wrapping yarn around the needle 2 times for every stitch (see page 170).
Row 2 Purl into sts, dropping wrap off needle.

TUBE
Beginning with a RS row, work 7 rows in St st.
Close Tube Turn work (WS facing): * Slip 1 st from left-hand (LH) needle to right-hand (RH) needle; insert RH needle under strand running between first st and second st on first row of Tube; slip st on RH needle over strand; continue from * across Tube sts. At end of row, slip last st on LH needle to RH needle.

NOTES
1 See *It's Easy*, page 1, for Tubes and Splits. *2* Use 2 strands of slub (S) held together. *3* End each pattern stitch section with a wrong-side (WS) row. *4* When changing colors, work first row of a new color in St st.

Cardi
SLEEVES
With L, cast on 4 sts. Work Seed st, increasing 1 st at beginning and end of every row 15 (15, 16) times—34 (34, 36) sts. Work even for 1".
Begin increasing Increase 1 st at beginning and end of every 3rd row (except Tube rows) to top of Sleeve AT SAME TIME work patterns and yarns as follows:
Next 8 rows Work Basket Weave.
Next row (RS) With S, purl.
Next row With L, knit.
3" Splits Mark center 10 sts. With L, work SRS to center sts, turn, work back and forth on edge sts for 3", ending with a RS row (a section); with R, work a Seed-st section on next 10 sts; with L, work SRS section on remaining sts.
Next row (WS) With L, purl.

Tube With O, work Tube over all sts.
With L Work 4 rows St st, 2 rows Ladder st, 4 rows St st.
Next row (RS) With S, purl.
With L K 1 row, work in P4, K4 Rib for 4 (4, 3)".
Next 2 rows With R, work St st.
Next row (RS) With L, work Seed st to center 50 sts, k20, work 10 sts Seed st, k20, and work Seed st to end.
Next row (WS) Maintain Seed st and St st patterns, p into front and back of each St st (increasing 40 sts in row).
Next 7 rows Work even in Seed and St st.

Next row (WS) Maintain patterns and p2tog across each 40-st St-st section (decreasing 40 sts in row).
Tube With O, work Tube on all sts.
Next row (RS) With L, bind off loosely.

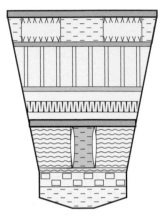

Cardi 11 (12, 13) balls MAGGI'S LINEN (L) in Natural; 2 balls MAGGI'S LINEN in Olive (O); 1 ball MAGGI'S MIST SLUB (S) in Beige/Olive; 1 ball MAGGI'S RAG (R) in Olive

BACK

Note Begin as 2 pieces, then join.

Right side

With L, cast on 10 (12, 14) sts. Work Seed st, increasing 1 st every row (at beginning of RS rows and end of WS rows) 42 (46, 46) times—52 (56, 60) sts. Work 1" even.

Next 5" Work 10 sts Seed st at beginning and end of row, work center 32 (36, 40) sts in SRS. *

Next row (RS) With S, purl.

Next row (WS) With L, knit.

Next row (RS) Work Basket Weave to last 10 sts, Seed st 10 sts. Work pattern for 3 (4, 5)".

Next row (RS) With O, work Tube to last 10 sts; with L, k Tube sts, work 10 sts Seed st.

Next row (WS) With L, work 10 sts Seed st, work SRS to end. Work pattern for 3". Leave sts on a spare needle.

Left side

Work as Right side to *, reversing shaping (increase at end of RS rows and beginning of WS rows).

Next row (RS) Work 10 sts Seed st, work SRS to end. Work pattern for 2 (2, 3)".

Next row (RS) With S, purl.

Next row (WS) With L, knit.

3 (4, 4)" Splits With L, work a 10-st Seed-st section; with R, a 10-st Seed-st section; with O, a 4-st Seed-st section; with L, a P4, K4 Rib section on remaining sts.

Join 2 pieces

Next row (RS) With S, p across both pieces—104 (112, 120) sts.

Next row With L, knit.

** **Next row** (RS) Work 12 (16, 20) sts Seed st, k20, [work 10 sts Seed st, k20] 2 times, work 12 (16, 20) sts Seed st.

Next row Maintain Seed st and St st patterns, p into front and back of each St st (increasing 60 sts in row)—164 (172, 180) sts.

Next 7 rows Work even in Seed st and St st.

Next row (WS) Maintain patterns and p2tog across each 40-st St-st section (decreasing 60 sts in row)—104 (112, 120) sts. **

Next row (RS) With S, purl.

Next row (WS) With L, knit.

3" Splits With L, work a 24-st SRS section; with R, a 10-st Seed-st section; with L, a 4-st Seed-st section; with R, a 10-st Seed-st section; with L, an SRS section on remaining sts.

Next row (WS) With L, purl.

Next row (RS) With S, purl.

Next row (WS) With L, knit.

With L Work 2 rows St st, 2 rows Ladder st, 2 rows St st.

Tube With O, work Tube over all sts.

With L Repeat from ** to **.

Tube With O, work Tube over all sts.

Next row (RS) With L, knit.

Next 4 (5, 6)" With L, work P4, K4 Rib.

Next 2" Work Basket Weave.

Next 2 rows Work Ladder st.

Next 2" Work Seed st.

Work St st 2 rows O, 2 rows L.

Next 2 rows Work Ladder st.

Work St st 2 rows L, 2 rows O, 6 rows L.

Next 2" Work Seed st.

Bind off 38 (41, 43) sts at beginning of next 2 rows. Bind off remaining sts.

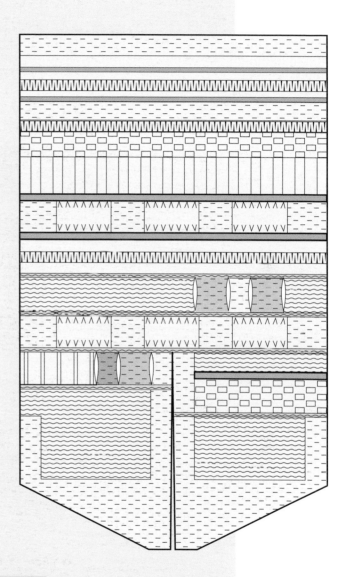

RIGHT FRONT

Work as Back, right side to *, reversing shaping.

Begin border Keeping 10 sts at center front (at beginning of RS rows and end of WS rows; place marker) in Seed st with L, work remaining 42 (46, 50) sts in patterns and yarns as follows (unless directed to work ALL STS):

Next 4 rows (RS) Work SRS.

All sts, next row (RS) With S, purl.

All sts, next row With L, knit.

With L Work 4 rows St st, 2 rows Ladder st, 4 rows St st.

All sts, next row (RS) With S, purl.

All sts, next row With L, knit.

All sts, 2 (3, 3)" Splits With L, work 10-st Seed-st section; with R, work 10-st Seed-st section; with O, work 4-st Seed-st section; with L, work 18 (22, 26)-st P5, K1 Rib section; with R, work 10-st Seed-st section.

Next row (WS) With L, purl.

Next row With O, work Tube; with L, k Tube sts.

** Next row (WS) With L, work 11 (13, 15) sts Seed st, p into front and back of next 20 sts; work 11 (13, 15) sts Seed st (increasing 20 sts in row).

Next 7 rows Work even in Seed and St st.

Next row (WS) Maintain Seed-st sections and p2tog across 40-st St-st section (decreasing 20 sts in row).

Next row With O, work Tube; with L, k Tube sts. ******

Next 3 rows Work St st, AT SAME TIME, after 25", decrease 1 st at center front every 4th row on RS 14 (15, 17) times (by working Seed st border, then k2tog)—38 (41, 43) sts.

All sts, next row (RS) With S, purl.

All sts, next row With L, knit.

Next 4 rows Work St st.

All sts, next 2 rows Work Ladder st.

Next 4 (5, 5)" Work Basket Weave.

All sts, next 2 rows With R, work St st.

Next 4 (5, 5)" Work SRS.

Next row With O, work Tube; with L, k Tube sts.

Next 2" With L, work Seed st.

<< **All sts, work St st** 2 rows O, 2 rows L.

All sts, next 2 rows Work Ladder st.

All sts, work St st 2 rows L, 2 rows O.

Next 2 rows With L, work St st.

All sts, next 2" Work Seed st. (Adjust, if necessary, to equal Back length.) Bind off. >>

LEFT FRONT

Work as Back, right side to *.

Next row (RS) With S, purl.

Next row (WS) With L, knit.

Begin border Keeping 10 sts at center front (at end of RS rows and beginning of WS rows; place marker) in Seed st with L, work remaining 42 (46, 50) sts in patterns and yarns as follows:

Next 3 (4, 5)" Work Basket Weave.

Next row With O, work Tube; with L, k Tube sts.

Work as Right Front from ** to **.

Next row (WS) With L, work 10 sts Seed st (center front) and p to end.

2 (3, 3)" Splits With R, work 10-st Seed-st section; with L, work 18 (22, 26)-st SRS section; with O, work 4-st Seed-st section; with R, work 10-st Seed-st section; with L, work 10-st Seed-st section.

Next row (WS) With L, purl. AT SAME TIME, after 25", decrease 1 st at center front every 4th row on RS—14 (15, 17) times (by working to 2 sts before border, k2tog).

All sts, next 8 rows [With S, purl RS row; with L, knit WS row, work 2 rows St st] 2 times.

All sts, next 2 rows With S, purl RS row; with L, knit WS row.

Next 5" With L work P5, K1 Rib.

All sts, next 2 rows Work Ladder st.

All sts, next 2 rows With O, work St st.

Next 3" With L, work Basket Weave.

Work as Right Front from << to >>.

COLLAR

With O, cast on 190 sts. Work 1 row Seed st. With L, p 1 row, work Seed st for 4". Bind off 20 sts at beginning of next 8 rows. Bind off remaining sts.

MAKING UP

Secure Splits (see page 1). Sew shoulder seams. Sew Sleeves to body, centering Sleeve at shoulder seam. Sew side seams, leaving sides open below end of Seed-st border. Sew bound-off edge of Collar to jacket, centering Collar at Back neck and stitching evenly around neck and down each Front. Press seams lightly using a damp cloth.

Shoulder pads are recommended to be worn with this garment.

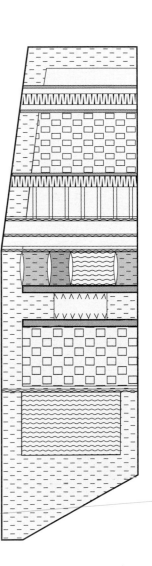

Yarns

☐ **L** natural linen

▨ **O** olive linen

▨ **S** beige/olive slub

☀ **R** olive rag yarn

Stitches

☐ Stockinette

▨ Seed

▨ SRS

▥ P4, K2 Rib

▥ AB Rib

▥ Basket Weave

☐ Tube

STANDARD FIT

Skill Intermediate

Fit Standard

Size S (M, L)

Approximate measurements

A 38 (42, 46)"

B side to underarm 14-15"

Apron 13" × 30"

Gauge 18 sts and 22 rows to 10cm/4" over Seed st with L

Yarn Medium weight

L 510 (630, 760) yds linen blend (waistcoat)
375 yds (apron)

O 125 yds linen blend (waistcoat)
125 yds (apron)

S 85 yds slub (waistcoat)

R 65 yds rag yarn (waistcoat)

Needles 5mm/US8, or size to obtain gauge; circular or double-pointed needles for I-cord (apron)

Extras Markers, five ¾" buttons (waistcoat), sewing thread and needle

P4, K2 RIB

RS rows * P4, k2; repeat from *.
WS rows K the knit sts and p the purl sts.

ALTERNATING BOBBLE RIB (AB Rib)

Row 1 (RS) * P5, k1; repeat from *.
Rows 2–4 K the knit sts and p the purl sts.
Row 5 P5, * work bobble by (p1, k1, p1, k1) in next st, turn, k4, turn, p4; p5, k1, p5; repeat from *.
Row 6 K the knit sts and p the purl sts, EXCEPT p the 4 bobble sts together.
Rows 7–10 Repeat Rows 1–4.
Row 11 P5, k1, p5, * work bobble in next st; p5, k1, p5; repeat from *.
Row 12 Repeat Row 6.
Repeat Rows 1–12.

TUBE

Beginning with a RS row, work 7 rows in St st. (See page 1.)
Close Tube Turn work (WS facing): * Slip 1 st from left-hand (LH) needle to right-hand (RH) needle; insert RH needle under strand running between first st and second st on first row of Tube; slip st on RH needle over strand; continue from * with Tube sts. At end of row, slip last st on LH needle to RH needle.

STOCKINETTE, SEED, SRS, and BASKET WEAVE

See page 62.

NOTES

1 See *Techniques,* page 170, for I-cord, cable cast-on, and ssk. *2* End each pattern-stitch section with a wrong-side (WS) row. *3* When changing colors, work first row of a new color in St st and bring new color under old color to prevent holes. *4* Cut rag yarn into 8" lengths and knot together, leaving 1" tails.

Waistcoat
LEFT FRONT

With L, cast on 14 sts. Work Seed st for 1½".
Cable cast on 14 sts at beginning of next RS row and continue Seed st on 28 sts for 1½". Cast on 14 (16, 20) sts at beginning of next RS row and continue Seed st on 42 (44, 48) sts for 1½". Cast on 8 (10, 10) sts at beginning of next WS row and continue Seed st on 50 (54, 58) sts for 1 (2, 2)".
Begin border Keeping 8 sts at center front (at end of RS rows and beginning of WS rows) in Seed st with L (place marker), work remaining sts in patterns and yarns as follows (unless told to work ALL STS):
Next 2 rows With O, work St st.
Next 1½" With L, work St st.
All sts, next 1" With S, work Seed st.
Next 4" With L, work SRS.
Next row (RS) With R, purl, keeping knots to RS.
Next row (WS) With L, knit.
Next 4" Work P4, K2 Rib.
***** **All sts, next row** (RS) Work 14 sts Seed st, continue rib, work border. Work pattern for 2".

Begin armhole shaping, all sts, next row (RS) Bind off 10 (14, 14) sts at beginning of row and work Seed st to end—40 (40, 44) sts. Work 1 row even.
All sts, next 4 rows Work Seed st, k2tog at beginning and end of RS rows—36 (36, 40) sts.
Add armhole border Keeping 6 sts at armhole edge (at beginning of RS rows and end of WS rows) in Seed st with L, and continuing to work k2 tog at neck edge 10 (8, 10) times—26 (28, 30) sts, work patterns and yarns on center sts as follows:
Next row (RS) With O, work Tube; with L, k Tube sts.
Next 4" With L, work SRS (beginning with Row 2).
All sts, next 2 rows With O, work St st.
Next row (RS) With L, k all sts. Work Seed st until armhole measures 7 (7, 8)". Bind off loosely. Mark center front edge for 5 buttons, one 1" above last cast-on, another at the beginning of neck shaping, and 3 spaced evenly between.

RIGHT FRONT

Work as Left Front until 50 (54, 58) sts on needle, EXCEPT cast on sts at beginning of WS rows 2 times, at beginning of RS row once. Work even in Seed st for 1 (2, 2)", AT SAME TIME, on RS row work a buttonhole to match bottom button marker on Left Front (work 3 sts Seed st, yarn over, k2tog, work 3 sts Seed st, work pattern to end).
Begin border Keeping 8 sts at center front (at beginning of RS rows and end of WS rows) in Seed st with L, work remaining sts in patterns and yarns as follows, working buttonholes to match Left Front markers:
Tube With O, work Tube; with L, k Tube sts.
Next 4" With L, work SRS (beginning with Row 2).
All sts, next 6 rows With O, work Seed st.
Next row With L, knit.
Next 4" Work in P4, K2 Rib (begin on WS row: k4, p2).
Next row (RS) With R, p to last 12 sts; with L, k12.
Next row (WS) With L, p12, k 30 (34, 38) sts.
Next 3" Work Seed st.
All sts, next row (RS) Work border 28 (32, 36) sts in P4, K2 Rib, 14 sts in Seed st. Work pattern to match Left Front length to armhole.
Continue as Left Front from Begin armhole shaping, reversing shaping, EXCEPT, instead of Tube, work 2 rows St st in S on all sts, and work last 2 rows of St st in S instead of O. Bind off loosely.

BACK & MAKING UP

Work as page 47, EXCEPT work Waist Tab with O.

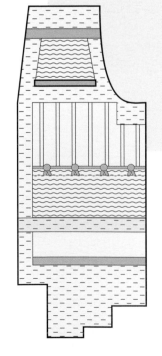

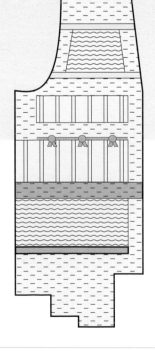

BOYLE CARDI, WAISTCOAT & APRON

Apron

SIDE PIECES (make 2)

With L, cast on 10 sts. Work Seed st for 29½".

Work eyelets [K1, p1, k2tog, yo] 2 times, k1, p1.

Work Seed st to 30".
Bind off loosely.

CENTER PANEL

With L, cast on 44 sts. Work Seed st for 2".

* **Next 3½"** Keeping 12 sts at beginning and end of row in Seed st, work 20 sts SRS. *

< **Next row** (RS) With O, work 22 sts Seed st, with L, work Seed st to end. Work pattern for 2". >

** **Next 3½"** Keeping 12 sts at beginning and end of row in Seed st, work center 20 sts AB Rib. **

Work < to >, reversing colors.

Next 3½" Keeping 12 sts at beginning and end of row in Seed st, work center 20 sts Basket Weave.

Work < to >.
Work * to *.
Work < to >, reversing colors.
Work ** to **.
Work Seed st for 1½".
Work eyelets * K1, p1, k2tog, yo; repeat from *, end k1, p1.
Work Seed st to 30".
Bind off loosely.

CORDS (make 2)

With L, work 60" 3-st I-cord.

MAKING UP

Sew side pieces to center panel. Thread cords through eyelets, beginning at side pieces and ending at center of main piece, leaving 3" end. Tie ends of cords in knot. Press lightly using a damp cloth.

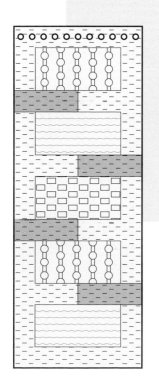

*Waistcoat 4 (5, 6) balls
MAGGI'S LINEN (L) in Natural;
1 ball MAGGI'S LINEN in Olive
(O); 1 ball MAGGI'S MIST
SLUB (S) in Beige/Olive; 1 ball
MAGGI'S RAG in Olive (R)
Apron MAGGI'S LINEN: 3 balls
in Natural (L), 1 ball in Olive (O)*

Yarns

- **L** natural linen
- **R** ivory ribbon
- **C** cream linen

Stitches

- Stockinette
- Seed
- SRS
- AB Rib
- Basket Weave
- Big Basket Weave
- Tube

Skills Intermediate

Approximate measurements Hem to hem 92"

Gauge 18 sts and 22 rows to 10cm/4" over Seed st in L

Yarn Medium weight

L 1820 yds linen blend

R 95 yds ribbon

C 126 yds linen blend

Needles 5mm/US8, or size to obtain gauge

Extras Markers

SINGLE RIDGE STITCH (SRS)

Rows 1 and 3 (RS) Knit.
Rows 2 and 4 (WS) Purl.
Rows 5 and 6 Purl.
Rows 7 and 9 Knit.
Row 8 Purl.
Row 10 Knit.
Repeat Rows 1–10.

ALTERNATING BOBBLE RIB (AB Rib)

Row 1 (RS) * P5, k1; repeat from *.
Rows 2–4 K the knit sts and p the purl sts.
Row 5 P5, * work Bobble [(p1, k1, p1, k1) in next st, turn, k4, turn, p4], p5, k1, p5; repeat from *.
Row 6 K the knit sts and p the purl sts, EXCEPT p the 4 Bobble sts together.
Rows 7–10 Repeat Rows 1–4.
Row 11 P5, k1, p5; * work Bobble in next st; p5, k1, p5; repeat from *.
Row 12 Repeat Row 6.
Repeat Rows 1–12.

BASKET WEAVE

Row 1 (RS) * K4, p4; repeat from *.
Rows 2–4 K the knit sts and p the purl sts.
Row 5 * P4, k4; repeat from *.
Rows 6–8 K the knit sts and p the purl sts.
Repeat Rows 1–8.

BIG BASKET WEAVE

Row 1 (RS) * K8, p8; repeat from *.
Rows 2–8 K the knit sts and p the purl sts.
Row 9 * P8, k8; repeat from *.
Rows 10–16 K the knit sts and p the purl sts.
Repeat Rows 1–16.

STOCKINETTE, SEED & TUBE

See page 71.

NOTES

1 See *Techniques,* page 170, for cable cast-on. *2* End each pattern stitch section with a wrong-side (WS) row, unless directed to end with a right-side (RS) row. *3* When changing colors, bring new color under old color to prevent holes, and work first row in St st.

Throw
SMALL SECTIONS (make 2)

With L, cast on 120 sts. Work Seed st for 1½".

Begin Seed-st borders Keeping 10 sts at beginning and end of every row in Seed st with L (place markers; move after binding off sts), work remaining sts in patterns and yarns as follows (unless told to work ALL STS):

Next 11" Work 33 sts SRS, 34 sts AB Rib, 33 sts SRS.
All sts, next 2 rows With R, work St st.
Next 1½" With L, work Seed st.
Next 2 rows Work Seed st, binding off 20 sts at beginning of each row—80 sts.
Next 1½" Continuing borders, work center 60 sts St st.
Next row (RS) With L, k5; [with C, work Tube over 10 sts; with L, k20 (Tube sts and next 10 sts)] 2 times, with C, work Tube over 10 sts; with L, k15.
Next row (WS) With L, purl.
Next 2" Work Basket Weave.
Next 1½" Work Seed st.
Bind off loosely.

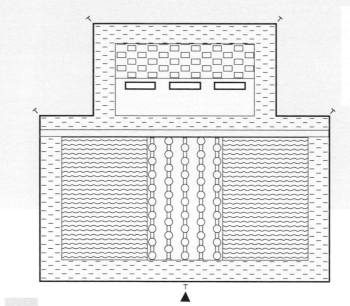

Throw 15 balls MAGGI'S LINEN (L) in Natural; 1 ball MAGGI'S RIBBON (R) in Ivory; 1 ball MAGGI'S LINEN in Cream (C)

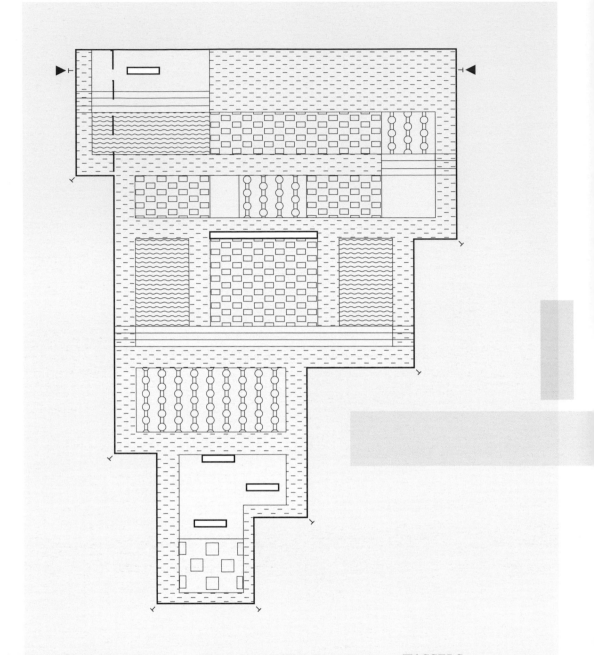

MAIN SECTION

With L, cast on 40 sts. Work Seed st for 1½".

Begin borders Keeping 8 sts at beginning and end of every row in Seed st with L (place markers, moving after cast-on sts), work remaining sts in patterns and yarns as follows (unless told to work ALL STS):

Next 24 rows Work Big Basket Weave.

Next 1" Work St st.

Next row (RS) With L, k5; with C, work Tube over next 14 sts; with L, k19 (Tube sts and next 5 sts).

Next row (WS) Purl.

All sts, next row Cable cast on 20 sts. Work these and next 8 sts Seed st, work St st to last 8 sts, work border—60 sts. Work pattern for 2".

All sts, next 1" Continuing borders, work 44 sts St st.

Next row (RS) With L, k5; with C, work 14-st Tube; with L, k to marker (Tube sts and next 25 sts).

Next 1" With L, work St st.

Next row (RS) With L, k25; with C, work 14-st Tube; with L, k19 (Tube sts and next 5 sts).

All sts, next row (WS) Cable cast on 16 sts. Work these and next 8 sts Seed st, work St st to last 8 sts, work border—76 sts.

Next 2" Work Seed st.

Next 6" Work 60 sts AB Rib.

All sts, next row (RS) Cable cast on 40 sts. Work Seed st to end—116 sts. Work pattern for 2".

All sts, next 2 rows With R, work 8 sts Seed st, 100 sts St st, 8 sts Seed st.

Next 6 rows With L, work St st.

All sts, next 2 rows With R, work 8 sts Seed st, 100 sts St st, 8 sts Seed st.

Next 8" With L, work 24 sts SRS, 6 sts Seed st, 40 sts Basket Weave, 6 sts Seed st, 24 sts SRS.

All sts, next row (RS) With L, cable cast on 20 sts. Work these and next 38 sts Seed st; with C, work 40-st Tube; with L, k Tube sts and work remaining sts Seed st—136 sts.

Next 2" With L, work Seed st.

Next row (RS) Work 20 sts St st, 30 sts Basket Weave, 29 sts AB Rib, 11 sts St st, 30 sts Basket Weave. Work pattern for 4".

All sts, next row (RS) With R, work 8 sts Seed st, 28 sts St st; with L, work Seed st to end.

All sts, next row (WS) With L, cable cast on 14 sts and work L sts in Seed st. With R, work R sts in pattern—150 sts.

Next row (RS) With L, work 20 sts St st, Seed st to end. Work pattern for 5 more rows.

All sts, next row (RS) With R, work 8 sts Seed st, 28 sts St st; with L, work Seed st to end.

All sts, next row (WS) With L, work Seed st to last 28 sts; with R, work pattern.

Next row With L, work 23 sts AB Rib, 70 sts Basket Weave, 41 sts SRS. Work pattern for 3".

* **All sts, next row** (RS) With L, work Seed st to last 49 sts; with R, work 41 sts St st, 8 sts Seed st.

All sts, next row With R, work 49 sts in pattern; with L, work Seed st. *

Next row (RS) With L, work 93 sts Seed st, 41 sts St st. Work pattern for 5 more rows.

Repeat from * to * once.

Next row (RS) With L, work 93 sts Seed st, k15; with C, work 11-st Tube; with L, k26 (Tube sts and next 15 sts).

Next row (WS) With L, p41, work Seed st to end.

This is the midpoint of the main section (arrow on illustration).

Work in reverse to beginning, binding off instead of casting on sts.

TASSELS

(Make 20)

Cut 10 lengths of L, each 16" long.

MAKING UP

Secure ribbon ends with matching threads. Center cast-on of Small Section along side of Main Section, matching midpoints and aligning with dotted line on illustration (Main Section overlaps Small Section). Sew. Press lightly using a damp cloth. Attach tassels to corners marked T in illustrations.

STOCKINETTE STITCH
(St st)
RS rows Knit.
WS rows Purl.

SEED STITCH
Row 1 (RS) * K1, p1; repeat from *.
Row 2 P the knit sts and k the purl sts.
Repeat Row 2 for Seed st.

TUBE
Beginning with a RS row, work 7 rows in St st (see page 1).
Close Tube Turn work (WS facing): * Slip 1 st from left-hand (LH) needle to right-hand (RH) needle; insert RH needle under strand running between first st and second st on first row of Tube; slip st on RH needle over strand; continue from * across Tube sts. At end of row, slip last st on LH needle to RH needle.

NOTES
1 End each pattern-stitch section with a wrong-side (WS) row. **2** Use white linen or another contrast yarn for center Tube, if desired.

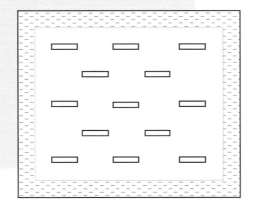

Yarns
☐ **M** ivory (or black) mohair
☐ **L** natural linen
☐ **O** optional contrast yarn

Stitches
☐ Stockinette
▨ Seed
▭ Tube

Skill Intermediate
Approximate measurements
Front 14" × 12"; Back 17" × 15"
Gauge 18 sts and 24 rows to 10cm/4" over St st with M using larger needles; 22 sts and 24 rows to 10cm/4" over St st with L using smaller needles
Yarn Medium weight
M 220 yds mohair
L 250 yds linen blend
Needles 5mm/US8 and 5.5mm/US9, or sizes to obtain gauge
Extras Markers, cushion insert approximately 13" × 13"; matching sewing thread

Cushion
FRONT
With M and larger needle, cast on 66 sts. Work Seed st for 1".
Begin borders Keeping first and last 6 sts in Seed st in M (place markers), work center 54 sts in patterns and yarns as follows:
Next 1" Work St st.
* **Pattern Row 1** (RS) With M, k2; [with L, work 10-st Tube; with M, k20 (Tube sts and next 10 sts)] twice; with L, work 10-st Tube; with M, k12.
Next 9 rows With M, work St st, starting with a WS row.
Pattern Row 2 (RS) With M, k12; with L, work 10-st Tube; with M, k20; with L, work 10-st Tube; with M, k22.
Next 9 rows With M, work St st, starting with a WS row.
Repeat from * once more.
Repeat Pattern Row 1 once more.
Next 5 rows With M, work St st.
Next 1" Work Seed st.
Bind off loosely.

BACK
With L and smaller needle, cast on 93 sts. Work Seed st for 2". Keeping first and last 10 sts in Seed st (place markers), work center 73 sts in St st for 12". Work Seed st on all sts for 2". Bind off loosely.

MAKING UP
Pin Front to center of Back, leaving Back borders loose. With L, stitch together, leaving opening. Press lightly using a damp cloth. Insert cushion. Stitch closed.
Black pillow only Using contrast yarn (red shown), make 3 long sts in each corner.

Cushion 2 balls MAGGI'S MOHAIR (M) in Ivory (or Black); 3 balls MAGGI'S LINEN (L) in Natural

Yarns

L natural linen

O olive linen

RAG MIX

Stitches

Stockinette

Seed

Cushion 1

Skill Easy

Approximate measurements
13" × 16" without frill

Gauge 16 sts and 22 rows to 10cm/4" over St st with 2 rows L, 2 rows T or R using larger needle; 18 sts and 24 rows to 10cm/4" over Seed st with L using smaller needles

Yarn Medium weight

L 375 yds linen blend

O 250 yds linen blend

M 85 yds slub

T 65 yds rag yarn

R 65 yds rag yarn

Needles 5mm/US8 and 5.5mm/US9, or sizes to obtain gauges

Extras 13 × 16" cushion insert

Optional ¼ yd of gold net or gold fabric

STOCKINETTE STITCH & SEED STITCH

See page 71.

NOTES

1 See page 1, for hand-knotting Rag Mix. *2* When knitting with Rag Mix, keep knots to right side (RS).

Color Sequence for hand-knotting Rag Mix: Cut thirty 10" lengths each of O, R, M, and T. Cut more as needed. (Optional addition: cut gold net or fabric into 10 × ½" lengths.) Knot strands together in following order: O, T, M, R, gold (if using), leaving 1" tails on knots.

FRONT

With L, and using larger needles, cast on 62 sts.
K 1 row (WS).
Next 13" Work Reverse St st (p on RS, k on WS), * work 2 rows in Rag Mix, 2 rows L; repeat from *, end 2 rows L.
Bind off loosely.

ADD FRILLS

Side edges With RS of Front facing and using larger needles and O, pick up and knit 44 sts along 13" side of Front.
Next row * K into front and back, k1; repeat from *—66 sts.
Work Seed st for 1".
Bind off very loosely.
Repeat on other side.
Top & bottom edges Work Frills on long sides, picking up 60 sts and increasing to 90 sts.

BACK

With L and using smaller needles, cast on 70 sts.
Work Seed st for 13".
Bind off loosely.

MAKING UP

Sew edges of pillow together, leaving an opening. Press lightly using a damp cloth. Insert cushion and stitch closed.

Cushion 1
MAGGI'S LINEN: 3 balls in Natural (L), 2 balls in Olive (O); MAGGI'S RAG: 1 ball each in Olive (R), and Tan (T); MAGGI'S MIST SLUB: 1 ball Beige/Olive (M)

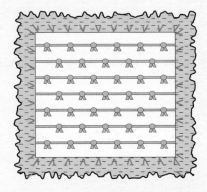

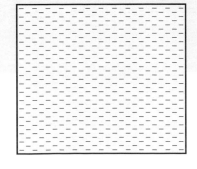

Cushion 2

Skill Easy

Approximate measurements
15 × 15"

Gauge 18 sts and 24 rows to 10cm/4" over Seed st with L

Yarn Medium weight

L 375 yds linen blend

O 125 yds linen blend

Small amount of Rag Mix from cushion 1 (approximately ½ oz)

Needles 5mm/US8, or size to obtain gauge

Extras Markers, 15 × 14" cushion insert

FRONT

With L, cast on 70 sts.
Work Seed st for 1½".
Begin Border Keep 10 sts at beginning and end of each row in Seed st in L (place markers), work center 50 sts in patterns and yarns as follows:
* **Next row** (RS) With L, k25; with Rag Mix, p25, keeping knots to front.
Next row (WS) With L, knit Rag Mix sts, purl L sts.
Next 1" Work St st.
Next row (RS) With Rag Mix, p 25; with L, k25.

Next row (WS) With L, purl L sts, knit Rag Mix sts. **
Next 2" Work St st.
Repeat from * 3 times, ending last repeat at **.
Next 1½" With L, work Seed st over all sts.
Bind off loosely.

ADD FRILLS

Right and left edges With RS of Front facing and using O, pick up and knit approximately 36 sts along inside edge of Seed-st border.
Next row * K into front and back of st; repeat from *—72 sts. Work Seed st for 1". Bind off very loosely.
Top and bottom edges With O, pick up 22 sts along top right half of pillow at inside edge of Seed-st border (see illustration). Increase and complete as above. Repeat for bottom right half. Sew corners of Frills together.
Center Frill With O, pick up 22 sts across left half of center of Front. Increase and complete as above. Sew Center Frill to left edge Frill.
Tassel Cut twelve 18" strands of O, fold in half. With large crochet hook, attach tassle in corner. Repeat for each corner. Trim ends.

BACK & MAKING UP

Work as for Cushion 1.

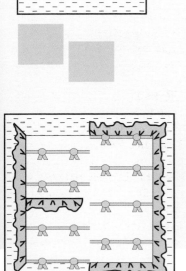

Cushion 3

Skill Easy
Approximate measurements
Knit piece 11" × 9"
Stuffed cushion 15" × 15"
Gauge 18 sts and 24 rows to 10cm/4" over Seed st with L
Yarn Medium weight
L 125 yds linen blend
O 25 yds linen blend
Needles 5mm/US8, or size to obtain gauge
Extras 15 × 15" finished cushion in natural or olive

FRONT PANEL

With L, cast on 50 sts.
Work Seed st for 1½".
Next 6" Work 10 sts Seed st, 50 sts St st, 10 sts Seed st.
Next 1½" Work Seed st.
Bind off.

EMBELLISH

Add Frill With RS facing and using O, pick up and knit 20 sts diagonally from one corner of St st area to the opposite corner.
Next row * Knit into front and back of st; repeat from *—40 sts. Work Seed st for 1". Bind off very loosely.
Weave * Cut five 20" lengths of O and weave in and out (1"-long stitches) along diagonal opposite Frill (see illustration); repeat from * 2 more times.

MAKING UP

Press lightly using a damp cloth. Sew Front panel to center of cushion.

STOCKINETTE STITCH (St st)
RS rows Knit.
WS rows Purl.

SEED STITCH
Row 1 (RS) * K1, p1; repeat from *.
Row 2 P the knit sts and k the purl sts.
Repeat Row 2 for Seed st.

SINGLE RIDGE STITCH (SRS)
Rows 1 and 3 (RS) Knit.
Rows 2 and 4 (WS) Purl.
Rows 5 and 6 Purl.
Rows 7 and 9 Knit.
Row 8 Purl.
Row 10 Knit.
Repeat Rows 1–10.

TUBE
Beginning with a RS row, work 7 rows in St st. (See page 1.)
Close Tube Turn work (WS facing): * Slip 1 st from left-hand (LH) needle to right-hand (RH) needle; insert RH needle under strand running between first st and second st in first row of Tube; slip st on RH needle over strand; continue from * across Tube sts. At end of row, slip last st on LH needle to RH needle.

NOTE
When changing colors, always work first row in St st.

TABLEMAT
With L, cast on 60 sts. Work Seed st for 2".
Begin borders Keeping 10 sts at beginning and end of every row in Seed st with L (place markers), work 40 center sts in patterns and yarns as follows (unless told to work ALL STS):
Next 4 rows With L, work St st.
All sts, next 2 rows With O, work 10 sts Seed st, 40 sts St st, 10 sts Seed st.
Next 4 rows With L, work St st.
All sts, next 4 rows With O, work Seed st.
Next 6 rows With L, work St st.
All sts, 1½" Seed-st Splits (RS; see page 1) With L, work 10 sts Seed st, turn, work back and forth in Seed st for 1½", ending with a RS row (10-st section); work 10-st sections in: R, O, R, O, and L.
Next row (WS) With L, purl.
Next 4 rows Work Seed st.
* **Next row** (RS) Work 20 sts St st, 20 sts SRS. Work pattern for 3 rows.
** **Next row** (RS) With L, k5; with C, work 10-st Tube; with L, k15 (Tube sts and next 5 sts); work 20 sts SRS.
Next 5 rows Work SRS and St st as established.
Repeat from **, EXCEPT end with 3 rows of SRS and St st. *
Next 4 rows With L, work Seed st.
Repeat from * to *, EXCEPT reverse placement of SRS and St st.
Next 4 rows With L, work St st.
< **All sts, Next 2 rows** With O, work 10 sts Seed st, 40 sts St st, 10 sts Seed st.
Next 4 rows With L, work St st.
Repeat from < 3 more times.
Next 2" Work Seed st.
Bind off loosely.

MAKING UP
Secure ribbon ends with matching thread. Press lightly using a damp cloth. Using a double strand of O, whip st each end of mat, placing sts about 1" apart.

Yarns

L natural linen
C cream linen
O olive linen
R ivory ribbon

Stitches

Stockinette
Seed
SRS
Tube
Whip Stitch

Skill Intermediate
Approximate measurements 12" × 16"
Gauge 18 sts and 24 rows equal 10cm/ 4" over Seed st with L
Yarn Medium weight
For 6 mats
L 1000 yds linen blend
C 125 yds linen blend
O 125 yds linen blend
R 95 yds ribbon
Needles 5mm/US8, or size to obtain gauge
Extras Markers, sewing thread

For 6 mats 8 balls MAGGI'S LINEN (L) in Natural; 1 ball each: MAGGI'S LINEN in Cream (C), MAGGI'S LINEN in Olive (O), MAGGI'S RIBBON (R) in Ivory

THE LINEN STORY
Flax still blooms in Ireland

(Far left)
The seeds whose fiber has clothed pharaohs, kings, and commoners.

(Left, top to bottom)
Gathering seeds for next year's crop—running a sheaf of flax through an iron-toothed comb.

(Below, left to right)
Eugene in his flax field; holding a tiny plant; showing seeds to a visitor.

(Facing page)
Flax flowers, "the wee blue blossoms."

THE LINEN STORY
Keeping an old craft alive

He still lives beside a small stream, a tributary of the River Lagan, whose waters once powered his father's scutching mill. Once its stations scutched up to two tons of flax fiber a day, but now the mighty water wheel is silent. "By the late 1950s the flax industry had moved to other countries," Eugene McConville says, "and no more flax was being grown in Ireland." For a visitor, Eugene will raise the sluice gate and allow the waters of the River Lagan to bring his water wheel to life. And, at least for a while, the giant, hundred-year-old wheel turns and Eugene is carried back to the time when flax bloomed in Ireland's fields.

"I'm doing this to keep an old craft alive," he says, then the sound of his voice is covered by that of rushing water…

(This and facing page, left to right) A lone figure walks beside his flax field; Eugene McConville's scutching mill in Dromore; a giant iron wheel comes to life, powered by the waters of the River Lagan; mill interior; cast-iron wheels and leather belts transfer the water wheel's power to the scutching shaft and its spinning blades of beech wood; newly scutched, fine flax; Eugene at a scutching station, separating the waste stalk from the flax fiber; crimping the fibers, the mark of good-quality flax; Eugene outside his mill—keeping an old craft alive.

(Top row, left to right)
Flax awaits scutching at Eugene's mill; tied stooks; stalks; scutched and dressed flax.

(From left)
Dressed flax hangs at the Dromore mill door — "You stroke the scutched flax with your right hand," Eugene says, "separating the fiber from any remaining waste, putting it in fine shape;" Eugene proudly holds his scutched and dressed linen.

(Facing page)
Once a common sight in Ireland, flax stooks at Eugene McConville's mill and 'flax museum.'

THE LINEN STORY
Irish Linen Centre & Lisburn Museum

The stooks of flax on the steps—
and the evocative 'Flax Pullers'
that hangs nearby—are harbingers
of the treasures inside the Irish
Linen Centre & Lisburn Museum.
Its brightly lit galleries are filled
with colorful exhibits, priceless
artifacts including a piece of linen
from King Tutankhamen's tomb,
prized oil paintings, and haunt-
ing audio-visual presentations.
In the darkened lower level of
the Museum, a piece of fine linen
hanging from the ceiling becomes a
screen—and a window into linen's,
and Ireland's, past (see photo,
facing page).
Lisburn grew from market town
to linen center with the arrival of
French Huguenots in 1698, at the
invitation of William III.

(This page, left to right)
*Images from the Irish Linen Centre & Lisburn Museum—Museum
exterior, Market Square, Lisburn; exhibition poster features the
'Flax Pullers' by Sir Ponsonby Staples, circa 1908 (Ulster Museum
Collection, MAGNI, courtesy of his estate); Victorian prayer chair
carved from Irish bog oak for Her Excellency the Countess of
Eglinton by Curran & Sons, Lisburn, 1852; a woman and young
weaver at a power loom; William Barbour, whose father John
established linen threadmaking in Lisburn in 1784; assembly
room; a 17th-century weaver with a bolt of linen; stooks of flax
on the Museum's steps—celebrating linen.*

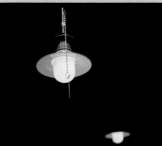

(Clockwise from left)
Factory lamps; 19th-century beetling
engine pounded linen cloth to give
it sheen; lacing cards for a jacquard
loom—it took six months to produce
one pattern; a jacquard damask
hand-loom; linen becomes a screen—
and a window into the past.

The linen industry was mostly 'women's work;' women made up three-quarters of the work force.

Shifts could last 12 hours, and children as young as ten or eleven worked at the mills part-time, attending school on alternate days. But it wasn't all work—'spinsters' advertised their availability by festooning colored ribbons on their spinning fibers: red, white, or pink meant she was single. Green or blue meant she was married.

(These pages, left to right)
A wedding garter in bobbin lace; drawn-threadwork lavender pillow or herb sachet; a dolly bag in pulled bobbin lace; replica of a linen store owned by Miss Weston, a milliner, dress, pelisse, and corset maker in the 18th century; flax spinner; red ribbons encircling the flax fibers of a 'spinster' advertise her availability; crochet samplers and pin cushions; 'Linen in Early Times' exhibit showcases a piece of linen from the tomb of King Tutankhamen, circa 1500 B.C.

SECTION 4 BROWNS

Yarns

L natural linen

B chocolate linen

C cream linen

Stitches

Stockinette

Seed

SRS

P4, K2 Rib

P5, K1 Rib

Basket Weave

Big Basket Weave

AB Rib

Tube

Skills Intermediate

Approximate measurements Length from shoulder to hem 24"

Width (from shoulder to longest point of large section) 45"

Gauge 18 sts and 24 rows to 10cm/4" over Seed st with L

Yarn Medium weight

L 1130 yds linen blend

B 750 yds linen blend

C 120 yds linen blend

Needles 5mm/US8, or size to obtain gauge

Extras Markers; large crochet hook

STOCKINETTE STITCH (St st), SEED STITCH, P4, K2 RIB, P5, K1 RIB See page 94.

SINGLE RIDGE STITCH (SRS)

Rows 1 and 3 (RS) Knit.
Rows 2 and 4 (WS) Purl.
Rows 5 and 6 Purl.
Rows 7 and 9 Knit.
Row 8 Purl.
Row 10 Knit.
Repeat Rows 1–10.

BASKET WEAVE

Row 1 (RS) * K4, p4; repeat from *.
Rows 2–4 K the knit sts and p the purl sts.
Row 5 * P4, k4; repeat from *.
Rows 6–8 K the knit sts and p the purl sts.
Repeat Rows 1–8.

BIG BASKET WEAVE

Row 1 (RS) * K8, p8; repeat from *.
Rows 2–8 K the knit sts and p the purl sts.
Row 9 * P8, k8; repeat from *.
Rows 10–16 K the knit sts and p the purl sts.
Repeat Rows 1–16.

ALTERNATING BOBBLE RIB (AB Rib)

Row 1 (RS) * P5, k1; repeat from *.
Rows 2–4 K the knit sts and p the purl sts.
Row 5 P5; * work Bobble [(p1, k1, p1, k1) in next st, turn, k4, turn, p4], p5, k1, p5; repeat from *.
Row 6 K the knit sts and p the purl sts EXCEPT p the 4 Bobble sts together.
Rows 7–10 Repeat Rows 1–4.
Row 11 P5, k1, p5; * work Bobble in next st, p5, k1, p5; repeat from *.
Row 12 Repeat Row 6.
Repeat Rows 1–12.

TUBE

Beginning with a RS row, work 7 rows St st. (See page 1.)
Close Tube Turn work (WS facing): * Slip 1 st from left-hand (LH) needle to right-hand (RH) needle; insert RH needle under strand running between first st and second st on first row of Tube; slip st on RH needle over strand; continue from * across Tube sts. At end of row, slip last st on LH needle to RH needle.

NOTES

1 See *Techniques*, page 170, for cable cast-on and tassels. *2* End each pattern-stitch section with a wrong-side (WS) row, unless directed to end with a right-side (RS) row. *3* When changing colors, bring new color under old color to avoid holes and work first row of new color in St st.

Shawl
SMALL SECTION

With L, cast on 120 sts. Work Seed st for 1".
Begin Seed-st borders Keeping first and last 10 sts in Seed st with L (place markers; move after binding off sts), work remaining sts in patterns and yarns as follows (unless told to work ALL STS):
Next 9" (RS) With B, work 33 sts SRS; with L, work 34 sts AB Rib; with B, work 33 sts SRS.
Next 1½" With L, work Seed st.
Next 2 rows Work Seed st, binding off 20 sts at beginning of each row—80 sts.
Next 1½" Continuing borders, work center 60 sts St st.
Next row (RS) With L, k5; [with C, work 10-st Tube; with L, k20 (Tube sts and next 10 sts)] 3 times, ending k15.
Next row (WS) With L, purl.
Next 2" Work Basket Weave.
Next 1" Work Seed st.
Bind off loosely.

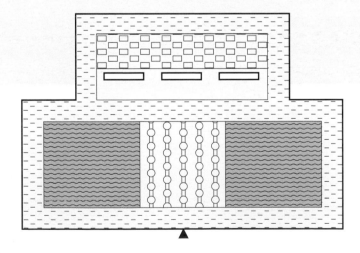

MAGGI'S LINEN: 9 balls in Natural (L), 6 balls in Chocolate (B), 1 ball in Cream (C)

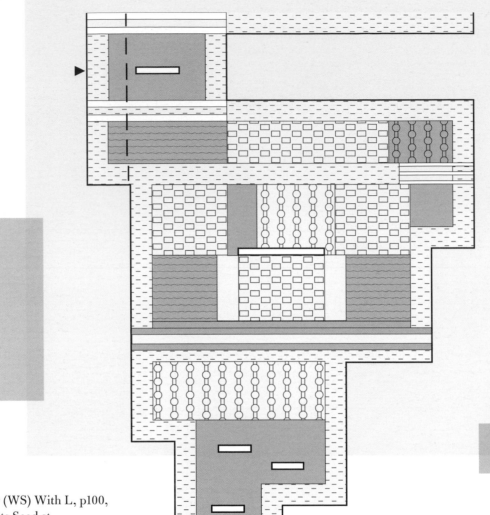

MAIN SECTION

With L, cast on 40 sts. Work Seed st for 1".

Begin Seed-st borders Keeping 8 sts at beginning and end of every row in Seed st with L (place markers; move after casting on sts), work remaining sts in patterns and yarns as follows (unless told to work ALL STS):

Next 24 rows With L, work Big Basket Weave.

Next 2" With B, work St st.

Next row (RS) With B, k5; with C, work 14-st Tube; with B, k Tube sts and next 5 sts.

Next row (WS) With B, purl.

All sts, next row (RS) With L, cable cast on 20 sts and work 28 sts Seed st (cast-on sts and border sts); with B, work 24 sts St st; with L, work border—60 sts. Work pattern for 2".

Next 2" Continuing borders, with B, work St st.

Next row (RS) With B, k5; with C, work 14-st Tube; with B, k Tube sts and next 25 sts.

Next 2" With B, work St st.

Next row (RS) With B, k25; with C, work 14-st Tube; with B, k19.

All sts, next row (WS) With L, cast on 16 sts and work 24 sts Seed st; with B, work 44 sts St st; with L, work border—76 sts. Work pattern for 2".

Next 5" With L, work AB Rib.

All sts, next row (RS) Cast on 40 sts and work Seed st on all 116 sts. Work pattern for 2".

All sts, Work St st, 2 rows B, 6 rows L, 2 rows B.

Next 7" With B, work 24 sts SRS; with L, work 6 sts St st, 40 sts Basket Weave, 6 sts St st; with B, work 24 sts SRS.

All sts, next row (RS) With L, cast on 20 sts and work 28 sts Seed st, k30; with C, work 40-st Tube; with L, k Tube sts and k to border, work border—136 sts.

Next row (WS) With L, p100, work 20 sts Seed st.

Next row (RS) With L, work 20 sts Seed st; work 30 sts Basket Weave; 29 sts AB Rib; with B, work 11 sts St st; with L, work 30 sts Basket Weave. Work pattern for 2".

Next row (RS) With B, work 20 sts St st; with L and B, work rest of row as established. Work pattern for 3".

Next row (RS) With C, k20 sts; with L, work Seed st.

All sts, next row (WS) With L, cast on 14 sts and work Seed st to last 28 sts; with C, p28—150 sts.

Next row With L, work 20 sts St st, work Seed st to end. Work pattern for 9 more rows.

All sts, next row (RS) With C, k28; with L, work Seed st to end.

All sts, next row With L, work L sts in Seed st; with C, purl C sts.

Next row (RS) With B, work 23 sts AB Rib; with L, work 70 sts Basket Weave; with B, work 41 sts SRS. Work pattern for 3".

* All sts, next row (RS) With L, work Seed st to last 49 sts; with C, k49.

All sts, next row (WS) With C, purl C sts; with L, work L sts in Seed st. *

All sts, next row (RS) With L, work Seed st to last 49 sts, work 41

sts St st, 8 sts Seed st. Work pattern for 7 rows.

Repeat from * to * once.

Neck opening, all sts, next row (RS) With L, bind off 104 sts loosely, work Seed st to end—46 sts.

Next 2½" With B, work St st.

Next row (RS) With B, k12; with C, work 16-st Tube; with B, k28 (Tube sts and next 12 sts).

Next row With B, work St st. This is the midpoint of the main section (arrow on illustration). Work in reverse to beginning, binding off instead of casting on sts.

TASSELS
(Make 19)
Cut 10 lengths of L, each 16" long.

MAKING UP
Center cast-on edge of Small Section along side of Main Section at black triangle and sew. Press edges lightly using a damp cloth. Attach tassels to corners and at center of Main piece (black triangle on diagram).

Can be worn over one shoulder or both.

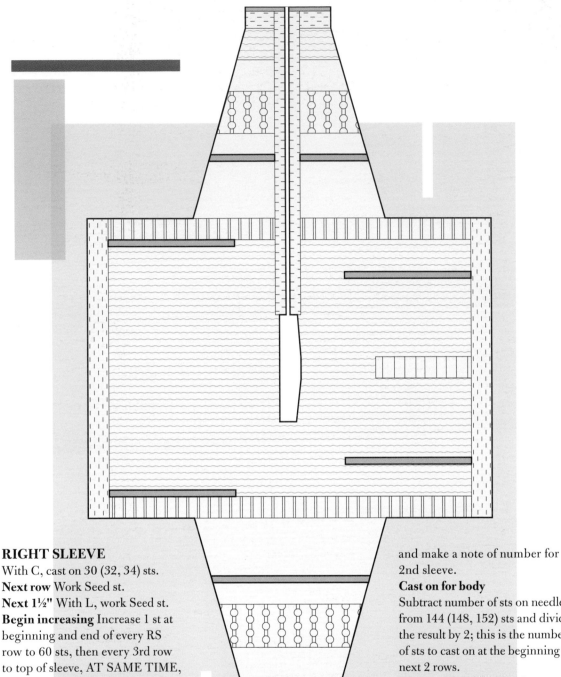

STOCKINETTE STITCH
(St st)
RS rows Knit.
WS rows Purl.

SEED STITCH
Row 1 * K1, p1; repeat from *.
Row 2 P the knit sts and k the purl sts.
Repeat Row 2 for Seed st.

SRS, AB RIB See page 90.

P4, K2 RIB
Row 1 (RS) * P4, k2; repeat from *.
Row 2 K the knit sts and p the purl sts.
Repeat Row 2 for Rib.

P5, K1 RIB
Row 1 (RS) * P5, k1; repeat from *.
Row 2 P the purl sts and k the knit sts.
Repeat Row 2 for Rib.

TUBE
Beginning with a RS row, work 7 rows in St st. (See page 1.)
Close Tube Turn work (WS facing): * Slip 1 st from left-hand (LH) needle to right-hand (RH) needle; insert RH needle under strand running between first st and second st on first row of Tube; slip st on RH needle over strand; continue from * across Tube sts. At end of row, slip last st on LH needle to RH needle.

NOTES
1 See *Techniques,* page 170, for cable cast-on. *2* Sweater is knit in one piece from cuff to cuff. *3* End each pattern-stitch section with a wrong-side (WS) row. *4* When changing colors, bring new color under old color to prevent holes, and work first row in St st.

Yarns

L *natural linen*

C *chocolate linen*

Stitches

Stockinette

Seed

SRS

AB Rib

P4, K2 Rib

P5, K1 Rib

Tube

C
B **A**
LOOSE FIT

Skill Intermediate
Fit Loose
Size S (M, L)
Approximate measurements
A 43 (45, 49)"
B 17 (17½, 18)"
C 29 (30, 30½)"
Gauge 18 sts and 24 rows to 10cm/4" over St st
Yarn Medium weight
L 1260 (1386, 1512) yds linen blend
C 126 yds linen blend
Needles 5mm/US8, or size to obtain gauge
Extras 9 buttons and st marker

RIGHT SLEEVE
With C, cast on 30 (32, 34) sts.
Next row Work Seed st.
Next 1½" With L, work Seed st.
Begin increasing Increase 1 st at beginning and end of every RS row to 60 sts, then every 3rd row to top of sleeve, AT SAME TIME, working patterns and yarns as follows (note numbers of increases for 2nd sleeve):
Next 3" With L, work SRS.
Next 2" Work St st.
Next 4" Work AB Rib.
Next 3" Work St st.
Tube With C, work Tube over all sts.
Next 4" With L, work St st. Sleeve should measure approximately 18". Count sts on needle

and make a note of number for 2nd sleeve.
Cast on for body
Subtract number of sts on needle from 144 (148, 152) sts and divide the result by 2; this is the number of sts to cast on at the beginning of next 2 rows.
Next 2 rows With L, cable cast on required number of sts at beginning of row, work P4, K2 Rib to end—144 (148, 152) sts.
Next 2 (2, 3)" Continue in P4, K2 Rib.
Next row (RS) With L, k to last 50 sts; with C, work Tube over 50 sts; with L, k to end.
Next row (WS) With L, purl.
Next 3" Work SRS.

Next row (RS) With C, work Tube over 40 sts; with L, k40, continue SRS to end.

Next 2" With L, SRS.

Divide for neck

Next row (RS) Work SRS over 69 (71, 73) sts, turn and work back and forth on these sts only for Front of sweater, placing remaining 75 (77, 79) sts on hold for Back.

Next 2 (3, 3)" Work SRS, AT SAME TIME, p2tog at neck edge (beginning of WS rows) 5 times— 64 (66, 68) sts.

Next row (RS) Work P5, K1 Rib over 32 (33, 34) sts; work SRS to end. Work pattern for 3½ (2½, 2½)".

Next 2 (3, 3)" Work SRS, AT SAME TIME, increase 1 st at neck edge (end of RS rows) 5 times—69 (71, 73) sts.

Next row (WS) With L, cable cast on 6 sts, work 8 sts Seed st, SRS to end—75 (77, 79) sts. Work pattern for 3".

Begin border Keeping 8 sts at end of RS rows and beginning of WS rows in Seed st with L (place marker), work remaining sts in patterns and yarns as follows:

Tube With C, work Tube over 60 sts; with L, k 60, continue SRS to end.

Next 2" With L, work SRS.

Next 2 (2, 3)" Work K2, P4 Rib.

Next row (RS) Bind off the number of sts cast on for the Front, work pattern to end.

Front half-sleeve Keeping border sts in Seed st, work to match first Sleeve, decreasing at side only (beginning of RS row, end of WS row). With C, bind off loosely.

Begin Back

Next row (RS) With L, bind off 6 sts (neck edge)—69 (71, 73) sts. Work SRS for 7½ (8½, 8½)".

Next row (RS) Cable cast on 6 sts, work 8 sts Seed st (border; place marker) work SRS to end.

Next 5" Work SRS.

Next row (RS) With L, k19 (21, 23) sts; with C, work Tube over 40 sts; with L, k40.

Next 2" With L, work K2, P4 Rib (beginning on WS: p2, k4), AT SAME TIME, on last (WS) row, bind off the number of sts cast on for the Back, work pattern to end.

Back half-sleeve Work as Front half-sleeve, reversing decreasing (end of RS row, beginning of WS row) and border.

FRONT AND BACK BORDERS

With L and RS of Back facing, pick up and k 94 (98 102) sts. Work Seed st for 2". (Adjust length here, if desired.) Bind off loosely. Repeat for Front Border.

NECK BAND

With L, RS of sweater facing, and beginning at left side neck opening (including 8 Seed sts), pick up and k 80 (84, 88) sts around Front neck, right side neck, Back neck, ending before 8 Seed sts. Work k1, p1 rib for 5 rows; p 1 row, work k1, p1 rib for 5 rows. Bind off loosely.

BACK FRILL

With L, cast on 100 sts. Work Seed st for 1".

Next row K2tog across—50 sts. Bind off tightly.

FRONT FRILLS (make 2)

With L, cast on 130 sts. Work Seed st for 2½".

Next row K2tog across—65 sts. Bind off tightly.

MAKING UP

Sew right underarm seam.

Attach Back frill to center Back (approximately 11" above border) and sew across top of frill to keep in place.

Attach front frills from neck to border at either side of center and sew across top 1" to keep in place.

Left sleeve buttons

Lap 8 Seed sts of back half-sleeve under 8 Seed sts of front half-sleeve and sew at neck rib. Pin overlap along Sleeve and mark for buttons: one ½" from top, another ½" from bottom, and the others spaced evenly between. Sew buttons in place through both layers of Seed st.

Sew left underarm seam.

Fold neck rib to inside along purl ridge and sew loosely. (Doubled elastic thread may be woven through sts on WS to keep shape.) Press seams using a damp cloth.

Shoulder pads can be worn to give a slimmer image.

Sweater 10 (11, 12) balls MAGGI'S LINEN (L) in Natural; 1 ball MAGGI'S LINEN (C) in Chocolate

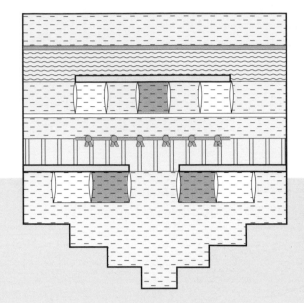

Yarns

T *beige tweed*

C *chocolate linen*

L *mustard linen*

R *cream ribbon*

 RY *chocolate rag knot yarn*

Stitches

Stockinette

Seed

SRS

P2, K2 Rib

P4, K2 Rib

Tube

Split

Cardi

Skill Intermediate

Fit Loose

Size S (M, L)

Approximate measurements

A 45 (49, 53)"

B from dip 23"

C 28½ (29, 29)"

Gauge 16 sts and 24 rows to 10cm/4"
over Seed st in T

Yarn Bulky weight

T 840 (840, 960) yds wool tweed

C 126 yds linen blend

L 126 yds linen blend

R 95 yds ribbon

RY 65 yds rag yarn

Needles 5.5mm/US9, or size to
obtain gauge

Extras Markers; five ¾" buttons

STOCKINETTE STITCH

(St st)
RS rows Knit.
WS rows Purl.

SEED STITCH

Row 1 * K1, p1; repeat from *.
Row 2 P the knit sts and k the
purl sts.
Repeat Row 2 for Seed st.

SINGLE RIDGE STITCH

(SRS)
Rows 1 and 3 (RS) Knit.
Rows 2 and 4 (WS) Purl.
Rows 5 and 6 Purl.
Rows 7 and 9 Knit.
Row 8 Purl.
Row 10 Knit.
Repeat Rows 1–10.

P2, K2 RIB

RS rows * P2, k2; repeat from *.
WS rows K the knit sts and p the
purl sts.

P4, K2 RIB

RS rows * P4, k2; repeat from *.
WS rows K the knit sts and p the
purl sts.

TUBE

Beginning with a RS row, work 7
rows in St st.
Close Tube Turn work (WS facing):
* Slip 1 st from left-hand (LH)
needle to right-hand (RH) needle;
insert RH needle under strand running between first st and second st
on first row of Tube; slip st on RH
needle over strand; continue from *
across Tube sts. At end of row, slip
last st on LH needle to RH needle.

NOTES

1 See *It's Easy*, page 1, for Tubes
and Splits and *Techniques*, page
170, for cable cast-on and tassels.
2 End each pattern stitch section with a wrong-side (WS) row,
unless directed to end with a right-
side (RS) row. *3* When changing

colors, bring new color under old
color, and work first row in St st.
4 Cut rag yarn into 8" lengths and
knot together, leaving 1" tails.

Sweater
SLEEVES

With T, cast on 30 (32, 32) sts.
Work 14 (14, 12) rows in P2,
K2 Rib.

Begin increasing Increase 1 st at
beginning and end of every other
row to 60 sts, then every 4th row
(except Tube row) to top of sleeve,
AT SAME TIME, work patterns
and yarns as follows:
Tube With L, work Tube over
all sts.
Next 2" With T, work SRS.
3" Seed-st Splits With T, work 14
sts Seed st, turn, work back and
forth in Seed st for 3", ending with
a RS row (14-st section); with C,
work a 6-st section; with R, work
a 6-st section; with T, work a section over remaining sts.
Next row (WS) With T, purl.
Next 3 (3, 2)" Work P4, K2 Rib.
Next row (RS) With RY, p26, keeping knots to RS; with T, k to end.
Next row (WS) With T, purl T sts
and knit RY sts.
Work St st With T, work 2½"; with
L, work 2 rows; with T, work 2½".
Next row (RS) With T, k to last 30
sts; with RY, purl to end.
Next row (WS) With T, knit RY
sts and purl T sts.

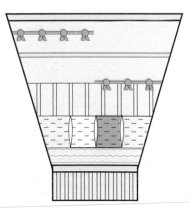

Next 1" Work St st.
Tube (RS) With L, work Tube
over all sts.
With T, bind off loosely.

BACK

With T, cast on 10 (10, 14) sts.
Work Seed st for 1½".
Cable cast on 12 (12, 14) sts at
beginning of next 2 rows, continue
Seed st for 1½"—34 (34, 42) sts.
[Cast on 14 (16, 16) sts at beginning
of next 2 rows and continue Seed st
for 1½"] 2 times—90 (98, 106) sts.
3" Seed-st Splits With T, work 14-
st Seed-st section; with R, work a 10
(14, 14)-st section; with C, work a
10 (10, 14)-st section; with T, work a
22-st section; with C, work a 10 (10,
14)-st section; with R, work a 10 (14,
14)-st section; with T, work last section over remaining sts.
Next row (WS) With T, purl.
Next row (RS) With L, work Tube
over 32 sts; with T, knit 54 (Tube
sts and next 22 sts); with L, work
Tube over remaining sts; with T, k
Tube sts.
Next 2" With T, work P4, K2 Rib
(begin on WS row: k4, p2).
Next row (RS) With T, knit to
center 50 sts; with RY, p50, keeping
knots to front; with T, knit to end.

Next row (WS) With T, purl T sts
and knit RY sts.
Next 2" Work Seed st.
Next 2 rows With R, work St st.
3" Seed-st Splits Mark center 46
sts. With T, work Seed-st section to
center sts; with R, work 8-st section;
with T, work 10-st section; with C,
work 10-st section; with T, work 10-
st section; with R, work 8-st section;
with T, work last section on remaining sts.
Next row (WS) With T, purl.
Next row With T, k to center 46
sts; with L, work 46-st Tube; with
T, k Tube sts and to end of row.
Next 3" With T, work SRS beginning with Row 2.
Next 2 rows With C, work St st.
Next 3" With T, work Seed st
(adjust length here if desired).
Bind off 36 (39, 42) sts at beginning of next 2 rows. Bind off
remaining sts.

Cardi 6 (6, 7) balls MAGGI'S TWEED
FLECK CHUNKY (T) in Beige; 1 ball each:
MAGGI'S LINEN in Chocolate (C) and in
Mustard (L), MAGGI'S RIBBON (R) in
Cream, MAGGI'S RAG (RY) in Chocolate

LEFT FRONT

With T, cast on 10 (10, 12) sts.
Work Seed st for 1½".
Cable cast on 12 (12, 14) sts at beginning of next (RS) row and continue Seed st for 1½"—22 (22, 26) sts.
[Cast on 12 (14, 14) sts at beginning of next RS row and continue Seed st for 1½"] 2 times—46 (50, 54) sts.
3" Seed-st Splits With T, work 20 (24, 28)-st section; with R, work 10-st section; with C, work 10-st section; with T, work 6-st section.
Next row (WS) With T, work 6 sts Seed st, purl to end.
Next row With T, k20 (24, 28) sts; with L, work 20-st Tube; with T, k Tube sts and work Seed st to end of row.
Begin border Keeping 6 sts at center front (at end of RS rows and beginning of WS rows) in Seed st with T, work patterns and yarns on remaining sts as follows (unless told to work ALL STS):
Next 2" With T, work P4, K2 Rib.
Next row (RS) With RY, purl, keeping knots to front.
Next row (WS) With T, knit.
Next 2" Work Seed st.
All sts, next 2 rows With R, work St st.
All sts, 3" Seed-st Splits With T, work 10 (14, 18) st-section; with C, work 10-st section; with T, work 10-st section; with R, work 10-st section; with T, work 6-st section.
Next row (WS) With T, purl.
All sts, Tube With L, work Tube; with T, k Tube sts.
Next 3" With T, work SRS, ending with a RS row.
Shape neck
All sts, next row (WS) Bind off 6 (6, 7) sts and purl to end—40 (44, 47) sts; border ended.

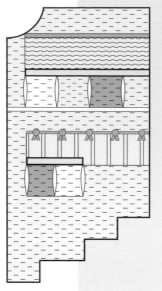

Next 2 rows With C, work St st.
Next 3" With T, work Seed st, k2tog at neck edge every other row 3 (4, 4) times; then work even on 37 (40, 43) sts.
Bind off loosely.
Mark front edge for 5 buttons, one at neck, another at bottom of first split, and 3 spaced evenly between.

RIGHT FRONT

Work as Left Front, reversing shaping and pattern placement, and on RS rows work a buttonhole to match each button marker on Left Front as follows: work 2 sts Seed st, yarn over, k2tog, work 2 sts Seed st, work pattern to end.

MAKING UP

Secure Splits (see page 1). Sew shoulder seams. Sew Sleeves to body, centering Sleeve at shoulder seam. Sew side seams above first Split. Press seams and front edges lightly using a damp cloth. Sew buttons to Left Front edge.

Shoulder pads are recommended with this garment.

Beanie
Skill Easy
Size One size
Finished measurements
22" circumference
Gauge 14 sts and 20 rows to 10cm/4" over Seed st using L
Yarn Bulky weight
T 120 yds wool tweed
L Small amount linen blend
Needles 6mm/US10, or size to obtain gauge
Extras Markers

BEANIE

With C, cast on 78 sts loosely.
Work 2 rows Seed st.
With T, work Seed st to 2" above cast-on edge.
Shape crown
Row 1 K11, k2tog, * place a marker, k11, k2tog; repeat from * across—72 sts.
Row 2 Knit.
Row 3 * K to 2 sts before marker, k2tog; repeat from *—66 sts.
Repeat Rows 2 and 3 until 12 sts remain. K2tog across row—6 sts.
Cut yarn, leaving an 18" tail, thread yarn needle and slip 6 sts from needle to yarn; pull tight. With remaining yarn, sew back seam.
Press lightly using a damp cloth.

Beanie 2 balls MAGGI'S TWEED FLECK CHUNKY (T) in Beige; small amount MAGGI'S LINEN (C) in Chocolate

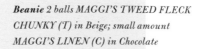

A turn-of-the-century, luxury hotel in Newcastle,
where the Mourne Mountains meet the sea.

Yarns

L *natural linen*

S *beige/grey slub*

Stitches

Stockinette

Seed

Ladder

P 1 row RS

T   Attach Tassel

CLOSE FIT

Skills Intermediate

Fit Close

Size S (M, L)

Approximate measurements

A 35 (37, 39½)"

B Top: 11½ (12½, 13)"; Dress: 30½ (30½, 31)"

C 19" (long sleeve), 15" (¾ length)

Gauge 15 sts and 22 rows to 10cm/4" over St st with 2 strands of L

Yarn Medium weight

L Linen blend, Top: 630 (750, 750) yds; Dress 1630 (1760, 1890) yds

S Slub, Top or Dress: 320 (400, 400) yds

Needles 6mm/US10, or size to obtain gauge

Extras Markers, sewing thread, 1½ (2, 2) yds 1" elastic, safety pin, additional yarns to mix into tassels (suggestions: Maggi's Rag in Tan and Maggi's Ribbon in Cream)

STOCKINETTE STITCH
(St st)
RS rows Knit.
WS rows Purl.

SEED STITCH
Row 1 * K1, p1; repeat from *.
Row 2 P the knit sts and k the purl sts.
Repeat Row 2 for Seed st.

LADDER STITCH
Row 1 (RS) Knit, wrapping yarn around the needle 4 times (3 for ¾ sleeve) for every stitch (see page 170).
Row 2 Purl into sts, dropping wraps off needle.

NOTES
1 See *Techniques,* page 170, for cable cast-on and tassels. *2* Use 2 strands of linen held together throughout. *3* End each pattern stitch section with a wrong-side (WS) row.

Dress and Top
SLEEVES
With S, cast on 26 (28, 30) sts.
Work 6 rows Seed st.
* Work 2 rows Ladder st, 4 rows Seed st. *
Repeat from * to * twice more.
Begin increasing Repeat * to * 7 times, AT SAME TIME, increase 1 st at beginning and end of every first Seed-st row—40 (42, 44) sts.
Work 2 rows Seed st.
Casing With L, work 6 rows St st.
Next row (RS) Purl. Work 6 rows St st. Bind off very loosely.

TOP BACK
With L, cast on 66 (70, 74) sts.
Work 1½ (1½, 2)" Seed st.
Work 10 (11, 11)" St st.
Work Casing as for Sleeves.

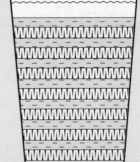

TOP FRONT
With L, cast on 10 sts. Work 2 rows Seed st. Continue Seed st, increasing 1 st at beginning and end of every row 24 times—50 sts. Cable cast on 8 (10, 12) sts at beginning of next 2 rows and continue Seed st on 66 (70, 74) sts for 1½ (1½, 2)". **
Next row (RS) Work 10 sts Seed st, 12 (14, 16) sts St st, 6 sts Seed st, 12 sts St st, 4 sts Seed st, 12 (14, 16) sts St st, 10 sts Seed st. Work pattern for 3".
Next row (RS) Work 22 (24, 26) sts St st, 6 sts Seed st, 12 sts St st, 4 sts Seed st, 12 (14, 16) sts St st, 10 sts Seed st. Work pattern for 1".
Next row (RS) Work 22 (24, 26) sts St st, 6 sts Seed st, St st to end. Work pattern for 1".
Next 1" Work St st.
Next row (RS) Work 40 (42, 44) sts St st, 15 sts Seed st, St st to end. Work pattern for 1".
Next 3" Work St st.
Work Casing as for Sleeves.

DRESS FRONT AND BACK
Work as Top Front to **.
Next 5" Work first and last 8 sts Seed st and center 50 (54, 58) sts St st.
Next 24" Work St st.
Work Casing as for Sleeves.
Bind off very loosely.

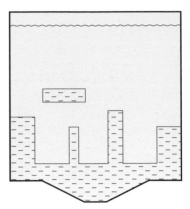

MAKING UP
Sew side seams, sewing above Seed st only on Dress.
Casing Fold Casing to WS along purl row at top of Body and stitch loosely, leaving an opening for elastic. Measure, cut and insert elastic (see page 1). Sew opening closed. Repeat for Sleeves.
Sew top of Sleeve casing to top of Front and Back casings for 3" at side seams. If desired, gather 3" at center Back for waist (2" up from bottom of Top; at waist for Dress).

TASSELS

Cut 8" lengths of S and L. Match other yarns that are thick and color coordinate with S and L. Fold in half. Working on RS of Top/Dress, use crochet hook to pull loop through where marked T (illustration below). Pull ends through loop and pull tight. Start at top and work approximately 1½" apart on main body but leave 2" untasseled at side seams. Make 6 or 7 rows, alternating tassels and yarns. Work tassels at top of Sleeve, leaving 2" untasseled at underarm. Scrunch tassels to give thicker look. Sew Sleeves to main body for 2" at underarm. Press seams lightly using a damp cloth.

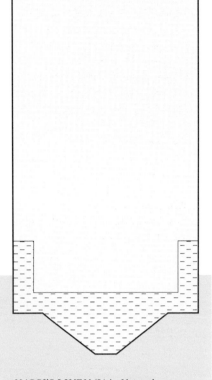

Detail of Top/Dress fold-over with tassel placement

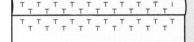

MAGGI'S LINEN (L) in Natural:
Top *5 (6, 6) balls,* **Dress** *13 (14, 15) balls;*
Top or Dress *4 (5, 5) balls MAGGI'S MIST SLUB (S) in Beige/Grey*

STOCKINETTE STITCH
(St st)
RS rows Knit.
WS rows Purl.

SEED STITCH
Row 1 * K1, p1; repeat from *.
Row 2 P the knit sts and k the purl sts.
Repeat Row 2 for Seed st.

SINGLE RIDGE STITCH
(SRS)
Rows 1 and 3 (RS) Knit.
Rows 2 and 4 (WS) Purl.
Rows 5 and 6 Purl.
Rows 7 and 9 Knit.
Row 8 Purl.
Row 10 Knit.
Repeat Rows 1–10.

NOTES
1 See *Techniques*, page 170, for cable cast-on. **2** End each pattern-stitch section with a wrong-side (WS) row.

BACK
Cast on 20 sts. Work 1½" Seed st. [Cable cast on 10 sts at beginning of next 2 rows and continue Seed st for 1½"] 3 times. At beginning of next 2 rows cast on 10 (16, 22) sts—100 (112, 124) sts
Next 2" Continue Seed st.
Next 9½" Keeping 10 sts at beginning and end of row Seed st, work 80 (92, 104) sts SRS.
**** Next 20"** Work SRS on all sts.
Begin decreasing at the beginning and end of every 6 rows 9 (0, 0) times, then every 4 rows 12 (24, 21)

times and then every other row 0 (0, 6) times—58 (64, 70) sts, then work 2 rows even.
Waistband, next row (RS) < Purl.
Next 7 rows Work St st; repeat from < once. Bind off loosely.

FRONT
Right side Cast on 20 (24, 28) sts. Work 1½" Seed st.
* Cable cast on 10 (12, 14) sts at beginning of next (RS) row and continue Seed st for 1½". *
Repeat from * to * once more—40 (48, 52) sts. Place sts on a holder.
Left side Work as Right side, but cast on sts on WS rows.
Join sides (RS) Work Seed st across Left side, cast on 20 sts, work Seed st across Right side—100 (112, 124) sts.
Next 2" Work Seed st.
Next 3" Keeping 10 sts at beginning and end of row in Seed st, work 80 (88, 96) sts SRS.
Work as Back from **.

MAKING UP
Sew side seams above Seed st (Front is 2" shorter than Back). Fold Waistband to WS at 2nd purl ridge and sew loosely, leaving an opening for elastic.
Cut elastic 3" less than waist measurement. Thread elastic through opening, overlap ends by ½", and sew securely. Sew opening closed. Press seams lightly using a damp cloth.

Stitches

☐ Stockinette

⊡ Seed

〰 SRS

〰 P 1 Row RS

STANDARD FIT

Skill Intermediate
Fit Standard
Size S (M, L)
Approximate measurements
A 44 (49½, 53)"
B 37" center front to waist; 49" center back to waist
C 25 (28, 30½)"
Gauge 18 sts and 22 rows to 10cm/4" over Seed st
Yarn Medium weight
1130 (1260, 1380) yds linen blend
Needles 5mm/US8, or size to obtain gauge
Extras Markers; 1 (1¼, 1¼) yds 1" elastic

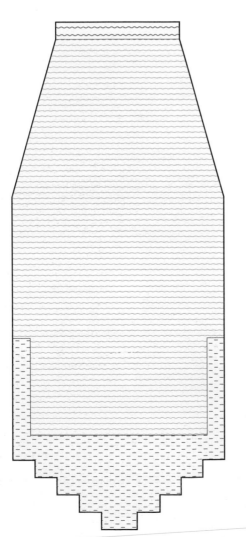

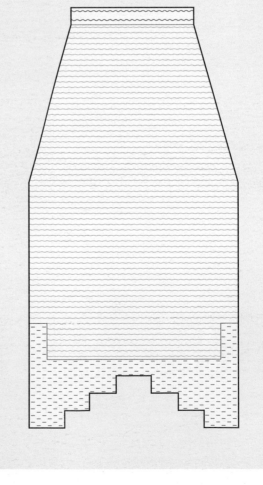

Skirt 9 (10, 11) balls MAGGI'S LINEN in Natural

STOCKINETTE STITCH (St st)
RS rows Knit.
WS rows Purl.

SEED STITCH
Row 1 * K1, p1; repeat from *.
Row 2 P the knit sts and k the purl sts.
Repeat Row 2 for Seed st.

TUBE
Beginning with a RS row, work 7 rows in St st.
Close Tube Turn work (WS facing): * Slip 1 st from left-hand (LH) needle to right-hand (RH) needle; insert RH needle under strand running between first st and second st on first row of Tube; slip st on RH needle over strand; continue from * across Tube sts. At end of row, slip last st on LH needle to RH needle.

NOTES
1 See *It's Easy,* page 1, for Tubes and Splits and *Techniques,* page 170, for cable cast-on. *2* End each pattern-stitch section with a wrong-side (WS) row, unless directed to end with a right-side (RS) row. *3* When changing colors, bring new color under old color to prevent holes, and work first row in St st.

Coat
BODY
* With L, cast on 10 sts. Work Seed st for 1½".
[Cable cast on 10 sts at beginning of next 2 rows and continue Seed st for 1½"] 2 times—50 sts.
Cast on 8 (10, 12) sts at beginning of next 2 rows and continue Seed st on 66 (70, 74) sts for 1".
Begin Seed-st borders Keeping 8 (10, 12) sts at beginning and end of every row in Seed st with L (place markers), work remaining sts in patterns and yarns as follows (unless told to work ALL STS):
Next 2 (4, 4) rows Work St st.
Next row (RS) With L, k10; [with C, work 10-st Tube; with L, k20 (Tube sts and 10 more)] 2 times.
Next 5 rows With L, work St st.
Next row (RS) [With C, work 10-st Tube; with L, k20] 2 times; with C, work 10-st Tube; with L, k10.
Next 5 rows With L, work St st.
Next row (RS) With B, k32; with L, k18.
Next row With L, p18; with B, p32.
Next 4 rows With L, work St st.
Next row (RS) With L, k18; with S, k32.
Next row With S, p32; with L, p18.
Next 2 (6, 10) rows With L, work St st. **
All sts, 2" Seed-st Splits With L,

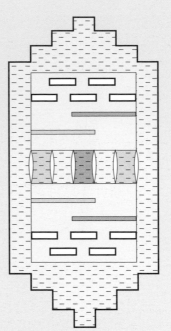

work 8 (10, 12) sts Seed st, turn, work back and forth on these sts for 2", ending with a RS row [8 (10, 12)-st section]; work 10-st sections of Seed st with S, L, B, L, then S; end with 8 (10, 12)-st section L.
Next row (WS) With L, purl. Work in reverse from ** to * for other half of body, binding off instead of casting on to last 10 sts. Bind off loosely.

TIES (make 2)
With L, cast on 2 sts. Work Seed st, increasing 1 st at beginning of RS rows and end of WS rows to 10 sts. Work even for 4 (6, 8)". Then increase 1 st at beginning and end of every row to 20 (22, 24) sts. Work even for 3 (4, 5)". Bind off loosely.

COLLAR
With B, cast on 50 (54, 58) sts.
Work Seed st With B, 1 row; with L, 2 (3, 4)".
Bind off loosely.

BRAIDS (make 2)
Braid three 7" strands of L. Tie a knot 1" from end.

MAKING UP
Secure Splits (see page 1). Attach braids to bound-off corners of Collar. Center Collar bind-off along edge of Splits and sew for 2". Fold back and sew corners of Collar cast on to form lapels. Sew bound-off edge of Ties to WS of Body, centering Tie along second row of Tubes.

Yarns
☐	**L** *natural linen*
☐	**C** *cream linen*
▨	**S** *beige/grey slub*
▨	**B** *chocolate linen*

Stitches
☐	*Stockinette*
⊡	*Seed*
⬭	*Tube*
◇	*Split*

Skill Intermediate
Size S (M, L)
Approximate measurements
Body width 14 (16, 18)"
Body length from tip to tip 20 (22, 24)"
Gauge 18 sts and 22 rows to 10cm/4" over Seed st with L
Yarn Medium weight
L 290 yds linen blend
C 126 yds linen blend
S 88 yds slub
B 126 yds linen blend
Needles 5mm/US8, or size to obtain gauge
Extras Markers

3 balls MAGGI'S LINEN (L) in Natural;
1 ball each: MAGGI'S LINEN in Cream (C),
MAGGI'S MIST SLUB (S) in Beige/grey,
MAGGI'S LINEN (B) in Chocolate

STOCKINETTE STITCH
(St st)
RS rows Knit.
WS rows Purl.

SEED STITCH
Row 1 * K1, p1; repeat from *.
Row 2 P the knit sts and k the purl sts.
Repeat Row 2 for Seed st.

K1, P1 Rib
RS rows * K1, p1; repeat from *.
WS rows K the knit sts and p the purl sts.

Top
SLEEVES
Cast on 2 sts.
Work Seed st, increasing 1 st at beginning of every row until 66 sts on needle.

Next 4 rows Continue Seed st, casting on 10 sts at beginning of rows—106 sts.
Next 3" Work even.
Next row (RS) K2tog across row—53 sts.
Next row (WS) * P2tog, p1; repeat from *, end p2tog —35 sts.
Next row (RS) K3, * k2tog, k6; repeat from * —31 sts.
Next 2" Work K1, P1 Rib.
Next row (RS) K1, * knit into front and back of st (kf&b); repeat from * to last st, k1—60 sts
Next row (WS) * P1, p into front and back of st (pf&b); repeat from *—90 sts.
Next 4" Work 8 sts Seed st (border), 74 sts St st, and 8 sts Seed st (border).
** Next row (RS) Work established patterns, decreasing 6 sts evenly across St st.
Next 7 rows Work even in pattern. ******
Repeat from ** to ** twice more—72 sts.
Next row (RS) K2tog across row—36 sts.
Next 2" Work K1, P1 Rib.
Next row (RS) Kf&b across row—72 sts.
Next row (WS) Work border, work St st, increasing 4 sts evenly across next 56 sts, work border—76 sts.
Next 4 (5, 5)" Work 8 sts Seed st, 60 sts St st, 8 sts Seed st.
Repeat from ** to ** 3 times—58 sts.
Next 6 rows Work Seed st on all sts.
Next row (RS) Purl.
Next 6 rows Work Seed st.
Bind off loosely.

BACK AND FRONT
Cast on 72 (80, 88) sts.
Work 6 rows Seed st.
Next row (RS) Purl.
Next 7 rows Work Seed st.
Next row (RS) * K1, kf&b; repeat from *—108 (120, 132) sts.
Next 9 (10, 11)" Work St st, ending with a RS row.
Next row (WS) * P1, p2tog; repeat from *—72 (80, 88) sts.
Next 6 rows Work Seed st.
Next row (RS) Purl.
Next 6 rows Work Seed st.
Bind off loosely.

LARGE ROSES (make 10)
Cast on 80 sts.
Work Seed st for 2".
Next row K2tog across row—40 sts.
Bind off loosely.

SMALL ROSES (make 6)
Cast on 70 sts.
Work Seed st for 1".
Next row K2tog across row—35 sts.
Bind off loosely.

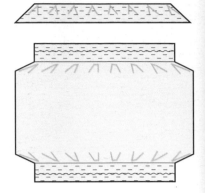

MAKING UP
Sleeves Seam K1, P1 Rib areas.
Front and Back Sew side seams.
Casing Fold Casing to WS along purl row at top and bottom of Body and stitch loosely, leaving an opening for elastic. Measure, cut and insert elastic (see page 1). Sew opening closed. Repeat for Sleeves. Sew top of Sleeve casing to top of Front and Back casings for 3" at side seams.
Roses Gather Roses along bound-off edge and curl into shape. Alternate large and small Roses on Sleeve tops, leaving 4 Large Roses to sew on Front and Back casing. Sew Roses securely to knitting but do not stitch through elastic. Press seams lightly with a damp cloth.

Stitches

□	Stockinette
⊡	Seed
▥	K1, P1 Rib
∿	P 1 row RS

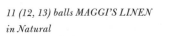

CLOSE FIT

Skill Intermediate
Fit Close
Size S (M, L)
Approximate measurements
A 32 (35½, 39)"
B 12 (13, 14)"
C 19" bloused
Gauge 18 sts and 22 rows to 10cm/4"
Yarn Medium weight
1380 (1510, 1630) yds linen blend
Needles 5mm/US8, or size to obtain gauge
Extras 1½ (2, 2) yds 1" elastic, elastic thread

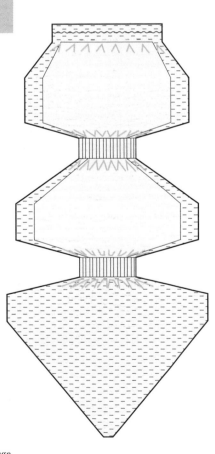

11 (12, 13) balls MAGGI'S LINEN in Natural

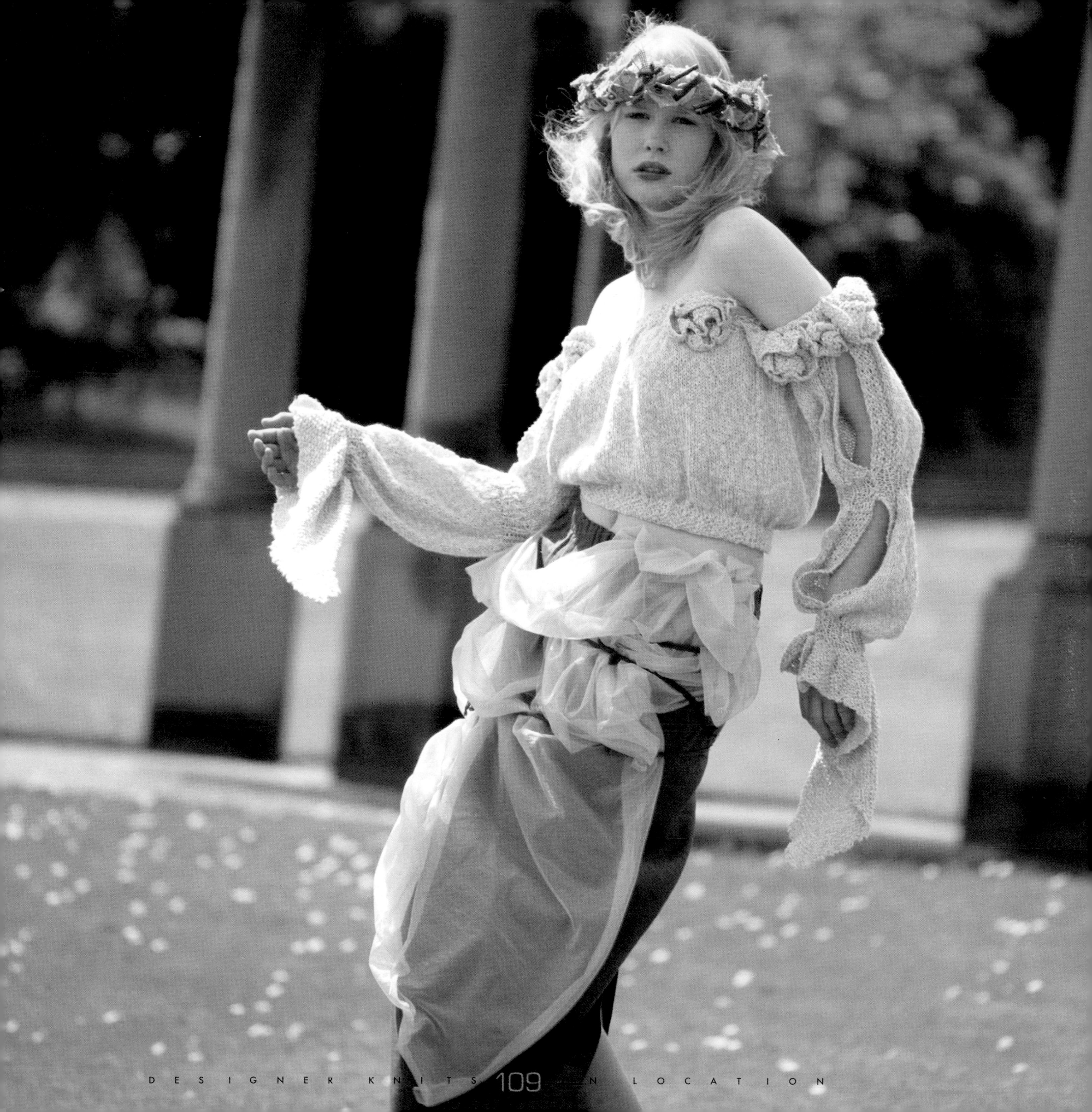

Yarns

- **T** black tweed
- **RY** tan rag yarn
- **R** black ribbon
- **O** olive linen
- **L** black linen/**RY** tan rag held together

Stitches

- Stockinette
- Seed
- SRS
- AB Rib
- P4, K2 Rib
- Ladder
- Tube
- Split

OVERSIZED FIT

Skill Intermediate

Fit Oversized

Size S (M, L)

Approximate measurements

A 50 (54, 58)"

B 23½ (25, 26½)" at sides

C 28½ (29½, 29½)"

Gauge 16 sts and 20 rows to 10cm/4" over Seed st with T

Yarn Medium weight

T 910 (1070, 1070) yds wool tweed

RY 135 yds rag yarn

R 95 yds ribbon

O 125 yds linen blend

L 125 yds linen blend

Needles 5.5mm/US9, or size to obtain gauge

Extras Markers; six ¾" buttons; sewing thread

STOCKINETTE STITCH (St st)
RS rows Knit.
WS rows Purl.

SEED STITCH
Row 1 * K1, p1; repeat from *.
Row 2 P the knit sts and k the purl sts.
Repeat Row 2 for Seed st.

SINGLE RIDGE STITCH (SRS)
Rows 1 and 3 (RS) Knit.
Rows 2 and 4 (WS) Purl.
Rows 5 and 6 Purl.
Rows 7 and 9 Knit.
Row 8 Purl.
Row 10 Knit.
Repeat Rows 1–10.

ALTERNATING BOBBLE RIB (AB Rib)
Row 1 (RS) * P5, k1; repeat from *.
Rows 2–4 K the knit sts and p the purl sts.
Row 5 P5; * work Bobble [(p1, k1, p1, k1) in next st, turn, k4, turn, p4], p5, k1, p5; repeat from *.
Row 6 K the knit sts and p the purl sts, EXCEPT p the 4 Bobble sts together.
Rows 7–10 Repeat Rows 1–4.
Row 11 P5, k1, p5; * work Bobble in next st, p5, k1, p5; repeat from *.
Row 12 Repeat Row 6.
Repeat Rows 1–12.

TUBE
Beginning with a RS row, work 7 rows in St st.
Close Tube Turn work (WS facing): * Slip 1 st from left-hand (LH) needle to right-hand (RH) needle; insert RH needle under strand running between first st and second st on first row of Tube; slip st on RH needle over strand; continue from * across Tube sts. At end of row, slip last st on LH needle to RH needle.

LADDER STITCH
Row 1 (RS) Knit, wrapping yarn around the needle 2 times for every stitch (see page 170).
Row 2 Purl into sts, dropping wrap off needle.

P4, K2 RIB
RS rows * P4, k2; repeat from *.
WS rows K the knit sts and p the purl sts.

NOTES
1 See *It's Easy*, page 1, for Splits and Tubes and *Techniques*, page 170, for cable cast-on. **2** End each pattern stitch section with a wrong-side (WS) row, unless directed to end with a RS row. **3** When changing colors, bring new color under old color to prevent holes and work first row in St st.

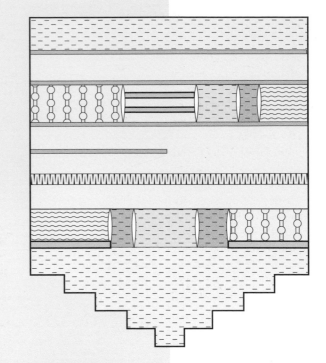

Cardi 6 (7, 7) balls MAGGI'S TWEED FLECK ARAN (T) in Black; 2 balls MAGGI'S RAG (RY) in Tan; 1 ball each: MAGGI'S RIBBON (R) in Black, MAGGI'S LINEN in Olive (O) and Black (L)

Cardi
BACK

With T, cast on 20 sts.

Work Seed st for 1½".

[Cable cast on 10 sts at beginning of next 2 rows and continue Seed st for 1½"] 3 times—80 sts.

Cast on 10 (14, 18) sts at beginning of next 2 rows and work Seed st for 3"—100 (108, 116) sts.

3" Splits with Tubes With O, work Tube on first 25 sts; with T, work AB Rib over these same 25 sts, turn, work back and forth in AB Rib for 3", ending with a RS row (25-st section); with RY, work 6-st Seed-st section; with L/RY, work 20-st Seed-st section; with R, work 6-st Seed-st section; with O, work Tube on remaining sts; with T, work SRS section on these same sts.

Next row (WS) With T, purl.

Next 3 (3½, 4)" Work St st.

Next 2 rows Work Ladder st.

Next 1" Work St st.

Next row (RS) With T, k40 (44, 48) sts; with RY, k to end.

Next row (WS) With RY, purl RY sts; with T, purl T sts.

Next 3 (4, 4)" With T, work St st.

Next 2 rows With RY, work St st.

3" Splits with Tubes With T, work 12-st SRS section; with R, work 6-st Seed-st section; with L/RY, work 14-st Seed-st section; work 22-st section as follows: * with T, work 6 rows St st; with O, work Tube over these sts; repeat from * once; with T, work 6 rows St st to complete section. With T, work AB Rib section on remaining sts.

Next row (WS) With RY, purl.

Next 3 (3, 4)" With T, work St st.

Next 2 rows With R, work St st.

Next 3" With T, work Seed st. (Adjust length here, if desired.)

Bind off 40 (44, 46) sts at beginning of next 2 rows.

Bind off remaining sts.

LEFT FRONT

With T, cast on 10 sts.
Work Seed st for 1½".
[Cable cast on 10 sts at beginning of next (RS) row and continue Seed st for 1½"] 3 times—40 sts.
Cast on 10 (14, 18) sts at beginning of next RS row and continue Seed st for 3"—50 (54, 58) sts.
Next 2 rows With T, work Ladder st.
Begin border Keeping 8 sts at center front in Seed st with T (at end of RS rows and beginning of WS rows), work patterns and yarns on remaining sts as follows (unless told to work ALL STS):
Next 2" Work SRS.
Next 3 (3½, 4)" Work St st.
All sts, next 2 rows With RY, work St st.
All sts, 3" Seed-st Splits With T, work 12 (16, 20)-st section; with L/RY, work 8-st section; with R, work 6-st section; with RY, work 14-st section; with T, work last section on remaining sts.
All sts, next row (WS) With RY, purl.
Next 2 rows With T, work St st.
All sts, next 2 rows Work Ladder st.
Next 3" Work P4, K2 Rib.
Next 3 (4, 4)" Work St st.
Next row (RS) With O, work 22-st Tube; with T, k Tube sts and k to end.
Check length Check that piece measures approximately 7–7½" less than Back to shoulder bind-off. Adjust length of St st that follows, if necessary.
Next 2" With T, work St st, beginning with a WS row.
All sts, 1½" Seed-st Splits With T, work 22 (26, 30)-st section; with R, work 8-st section; with L/RY, work 12-st section; with T, work last section on remaining sts.
Next row (WS) With T, purl.
Next 3 rows Work Seed st.

Shape neck
All sts, next row (WS) Bind off 10 (10, 12) sts and continue Seed st to end—40 (44, 46) sts; border ended.
Next 2½" Work Seed st, k2tog at neck edge every other row 4 times; work even on 36 (40, 42) sts until piece measures same length as Back to shoulder bind-off.
Bind off.

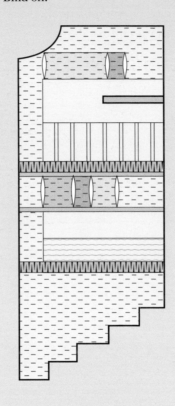

Mark front edge for 6 buttons, one at neck, another at ½" above bottom ladder section, and 4 spaced evenly between.

RIGHT FRONT

Work as Left Front, reversing shaping and pattern placement, and on RS rows, matching each button marker on Left Front, work buttonhole as follows: work 3 sts Seed st, yo, k2tog, work 3 sts Seed st, work pattern to end.

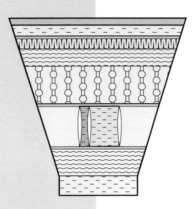

SLEEVES

With T, cast on 30 (32, 34) sts.
Work 2" Seed st.
Begin increasing Increase 1 st at beginning and end of every 3rd row (except Tube and Ladder rows) to top of sleeve, AT SAME TIME, working patterns and yarns as follows:
Next 3" Work SRS.
Next 2 rows With RY, work St st.
3" Splits With T, work a 16-st St-st section; with L/RY, work 10-st Seed-st section; with R, work 4-st Seed-st section; with T, work St-st section on remaining sts.
Next row (WS) With RY, purl.
Next 2 rows With T, work St st.
Next 4" Work AB Rib.
Next 2 (2, 1)" Work SRS.
Next 2 rows Work Ladder st.
Work St st 2 rows T, 2 rows RY.
Next 1" With T, work Seed st.
Tube With O, work Tube over all sts.
With T, bind off loosely.

MAKING UP

Secure Splits (see page 1). Secure ribbon ends with matching thread. Sew shoulder seams. Sew Sleeves to body, centering Sleeve at shoulder seam. Sew side seams above Seed st. Press seams and front edges lightly using a damp cloth. Sew buttons to Left Front.

Shoulder pads are recommended.

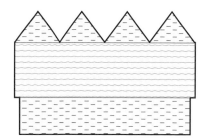

HAT
Cast on 76 sts.
Work Seed st for 4".
Next 5" Work SRS, knitting into front and back of every 6th st in first row—88 sts.
Shape crown
Work 4 triangular sections as follows:
Section 1 Working back and forth on first 22 sts, work 4 rows St st, then k2tog at beginning and end of every RS row until 1 st remains. Fasten off.
Sections 2, 3, and 4 Work as Section 1.

MAKING UP
Sew side seam and stitch triangles together. Press seams lightly using a damp cloth. Flatten top of hat into a circle and press flat. Roll hem and wear hat flopped to one side, keeping top flat, or wear as shown here.
Optional fur trim Seam sides of fur piece. Turn under narrow hem at top and bottom and sew. Pin or attach with Velcro to brim (stick adhesive back of hook side of Velcro to wrong side of fur). DO NOT PRESS FUR.

Stitches

☐	Stockinette
☐	Seed
☐	SRS

Skill Easy
Fit Standard
Size One size
Approximate measurements
22" circumference
Gauge 16 sts and 22 rows to 10cm/4"
over Seed st
Yarn Medium weight
180 yds wool tweed
Needles 5.5mm/US9, or size to obtain gauge
Extras Markers
Optional 22" × 3" faux fur, matching thread, stick-on Velcro

MAGGI'S TWEED FLECK ARAN:
Top *2 balls in Charcoal; 22" × 3" faux fur in Grey (shown with Galbally sweater, pattern on page 132)*
Bottom *2 balls in Black*

STOCKINETTE STITCH
(St st)
RS rows Knit.
WS rows Purl.

SEED STITCH
Row 1 (RS) * K1, p1; repeat from *.
Row 2 P the knit sts and k the purl sts.
Repeat Row 2 for Seed st.

LADDER STITCH
Row 1 (RS) Knit, wrapping yarn around the needle 3 times for every stitch.
Row 2 Purl into sts, dropping wraps off needle. (See page 170.)

NOTES
1 See *It's Easy*, page 1, for hand-knotting Rag Mix. *2* When knitting with Rag Mix, keep knots to right side (RS).

COLOR SEQUENCE FOR HAND-KNOTTING RAG MIX
Cut fifty 10" lengths each of L, G, M, S, C, RY, R, and B and knot strands together in this order, leaving 1" tails on knots. Cut additional lengths as needed.

TABLE MAT
With L, cast on 60 sts. Work Seed st for 1½".
Begin borders Keeping 10 sts at beginning and end of every row in Seed st with L (place markers), work 40 center sts in patterns and yarns as follows (EXCEPT when told to work ALL STS):
* **All sts, next 2 rows** With Rag Mix, work Row 1 of Ladder st. With L, work Row 2.
Next 8 rows With L, work St st.
All sts, next 2 rows With C and G held together, work 10 sts Seed st, 40 sts St st, 10 sts Seed st.
Next 8 rows With L, work St st.
Repeat from * 2 more times.
All sts, next 2 rows With C and G held together, work 10 sts Seed st, 40 sts St st, 10 sts Seed st.
Next 6 rows With L, work St st.
Next 2 rows With C and G held together, purl RS row and knit WS row.
Next 1½" With L, work Seed st.
Bind off loosely

MAKING UP
Secure ends of ribbon with thread. Press lightly using a damp cloth.

Yarns
L natural linen
C brown linen/**G** gold metallic held together
RAG MIX

Stitches
Stockinette
Seed
Ladder

Skill Intermediate
Approximate measurements 12" × 16"
Gauge 18 sts and 24 rows to 10cm/4" over Seed st with L
Yarn Medium weight
For 6 mats
L 1000 yds linen blend
C 125 yds linen blend
B 85 yds metallic
G 85 yds metallic
M 65 yds mohair
S 65 yds slub
RY 65 yds rag yarn
R 65 yds ribbon
Needles 5mm/US8, or size to obtain gauge
Extras Matching thread

For 6 mats 8 balls MAGGI'S LINEN (L) in Natural; 1 ball each: MAGGI'S LINEN in Chocolate (C), MAGGI'S METALLIC in Bronze (B) and Gold (G), MAGGI'S MOHAIR (M) in Ivory, MAGGI'S MIST SLUB (S) in Beige/tan, MAGGI'S RAG (RY) in Tan, MAGGI'S RIBBON (R) in Ivory

SECTION 5 SHADES OF BLACK

Yarns

 M *black mohair*

L *black linen*

W *white linen*

Stitches

Stockinette

Seed

Ladder

Whip st

OVERSIZED FIT

Skill Easy +

Fit Oversized

Size S (M, L)

Approximate measurements

A 44 (48, 52)"

B 53 (55, 55)"

C 34 (34, 35)"

Gauge 14 sts and 18 rows to 10cm/4"
over St st with Mohair

Yarns Medium weight

M 1540 (1760, 1980) yds mohair

L 510 yds linen blend

W 130 yds linen blend

Needles 6.5mm/US10½, or size to
obtain gauge

STOCKINETTE STITCH
(St st)
RS rows Knit.
WS rows Purl

SEED STITCH
Row 1 * K1, p1; repeat from *.
Row 2 P the knit sts and k the
purl sts.
Repeat Row 2 for Seed st.

LADDER STITCH
Row 1 (RS) Knit, wrapping yarn
around the needle 3 times for
every stitch (see page 170).
Row 2 Purl into sts, dropping
wraps off needle.

NOTE
End each pattern-stitch section with
a wrong-side (WS) row.

BACK
With M, cast on 76 (84, 92) sts.
Work Seed st for 3".
* Next 2 rows With L, work
Ladder st.
Next 4" With M, work 10 sts at
beginning and end of rows Seed st
and 56 (64, 72) center sts St st.
Repeat from * once more.
** Next 2 rows With L, work
Ladder st.
Next 4" With M, work St st.
Repeat from ** 6 more times.
Next 2 rows With L, work
Ladder st.
(Adjust length in next St st and
Seed st areas but work no less than
1" Seed st.)
Next 2 (3, 3)" With M, work St st.
Next 2 (3, 3)" Work Seed st.
AT SAME TIME, at beginning of
last 2 rows, bind off 28 (32, 36) sts
loosely. Bind off remaining sts.

Coat
SLEEVES
With M, cast on 56 (58, 60) sts.
Work Seed st for 4".
Next 2 rows With L, work
Ladder st.
Begin increasing Increase 1 st at
beginning and end of every 6th
row (except Ladder-st rows) to top
of sleeve, AT SAME TIME, work
patterns and yarns as follows:
* Next 3" With M, work St st.
Next 2 rows With L, work
Ladder st.
Repeat from * 3 more times.
Next 2 (1, 1)" With M, work
Seed st.
Bind off loosely.

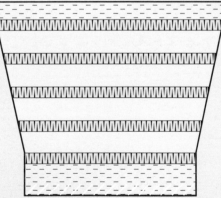

*14 (16, 18) balls MAGGI'S MOHAIR (M) in
Black; 3 balls MAGGI'S LINEN (L) in Black;
1 ball MAGGI'S LINEN in White (W)*

RIGHT FRONT

With M, cast on 40 (44, 48) sts.
Work Seed st for 3".
* Next 2 rows With L, work
Ladder st.
Next 4" With M, work 10 sts at
beginning and end of rows Seed st
and center 20 (24, 28) sts St st.
Repeat from * once more.
Next 2 rows With L, work Ladder
st.
Begin border Continue patterns
and yarns as for Back, keeping 10
sts at center front (beginning of RS
and end of WS rows) Seed st in M
sections.
AT SAME TIME, after 8th
Ladder-st stripe, shape for neck:
K2tog at beginning of every 4th
row on RS (except Ladder-st rows)
12 times—28 (32, 36) sts. Work
even until same length as Back.
Bind off loosely.

LEFT FRONT

Work as Right Front but reverse
center Front border (10 sts at end of
RS and beginning of WS rows) and
neck shaping (k2tog at end of row).

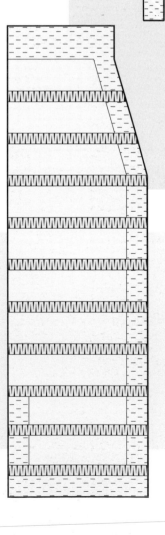

COLLAR

With M, cast on 8 sts. Work Seed
st for 7".
Continue Seed st, working
increases and decreases on right
edge of collar (at beginning of RS
rows) to shape collar as follows:
Increase 1 st every 6th row 10
times—18 sts, work 10 rows even;
k2tog every 4th row 6 times—12
sts, work 5" even; increase 1 st
every 4th row 6 times—18 sts,
work 10 rows even; k2tog every
6th row 10 times—8 sts, work 7"
even. Bind off.

MAKING UP

Sew shoulder seams. Centering
Sleeves at shoulders, sew Sleeves
to body. Sew sides above Seed-st
border. Sew Sleeve seams. Pin
center of Collar to center of Back
neck and sew to neck edge. Press
seams lightly using a damp cloth.
Turn cuff back at first Ladder-st
row and secure with a couple of sts
in M at side seam and again half-
way around.
Whip stitching With a large
needle and 2 strands of W, stitch
around cuffs and collar, stitching
about 1" apart and 1" deep.

Shoulder pads are recommended.

STOCKINETTE STITCH (St st)

RS rows Knit.
WS rows Purl.

SEED STITCH

Row 1 * K1, p1; repeat from *.
Row 2 P the knit sts and k the purl sts.
Repeat Row 2 for Seed st.

SINGLE RIDGE STITCH (SRS)

Rows 1 and 3 (RS) Knit.
Rows 2 and 4 (WS) Purl.
Rows 5 and 6 Purl.
Rows 7 and 9 Knit.
Row 8 Purl.
Row 10 Knit.
Repeat Rows 1–10.

ALTERNATING BOBBLE RIB (AB Rib)

Row 1 (RS) * P5, k1; repeat from *.
Rows 2–4 K the knit sts and p the purl sts.
Row 5 P5; * work Bobble [(p1, k1, p1, k1) in next st, turn, k4, turn, p4], p5, k1, p5; repeat from *.
Row 6 K the knit sts and p the purl sts, EXCEPT p the 4 Bobble sts together.
Rows 7–10 Repeat Rows 1–4.
Row 11 P5; k1, p5, * work Bobble in next st, p5, k1, p5; repeat from *.
Row 12 Repeat Row 6.
Repeat Rows 1–12.

TUBE

Beginning with a RS row, work 7 rows in St st. (See page 1.)
Close Tube Turn work (WS facing): * Slip 1 st from left-hand (LH) needle to right-hand (RH) needle; insert RH needle under strand running between first st and second st on first row of Tube; slip st on RH needle over strand; continue from * across Tube sts. At end of row, slip last st on LH needle to RH needle.

NOTE

End each pattern-stitch section with a wrong-side (WS) row, unless directed to end with a RS row.

Cardi

SLEEVES

With L, cast on 56 (56, 58) sts. Work Seed st for 4".
Begin increasing Increase 1 st at beginning and end of every 4th row to 78 sts, then every 6th row to top of Sleeve, AT SAME TIME, work patterns and yarns as follows:
Next 11" Work SRS to center 23 sts, work 23 sts AB Rib, work SRS to end.
Next row (RS) Mark center 35 sts. With L, k to center 35 sts; with B, work 35-st Tube; with L, k Tube sts and k to end.
Next 2 (2, 1½)" With L, beginning with WS row, work Seed st. Bind off loosely.

BACK

With L, cast on 20 sts.
Work Seed st, increasing 1 st at beginning and end of every row to 102 (108, 114) sts.
Work 1" even.

Next 5" Work 10 sts Seed st, work 29 (32, 35) sts SRS (place marker), work 23 sts AB Rib (place marker), work 30 (33, 36) sts SRS, work 10 sts Seed st.
Next 2 (3, 3)" Work SRS to first marker, 23 sts AB Rib, work SRS to end.
*** Next 2"** With L, work St st to first marker, 23 sts AB Rib, St st to end.
Next row (RS) With L, k9 (11, 12) sts; with B, work 20-st Tube; with L, k to first marker, work 23 sts AB Rib, k10 (11, 13) sts; with B, work 20-st Tube; with L, k to end. Repeat from * twice more.
Next 2" With L, work St st to first marker, 23 sts AB Rib, St st to end.

**** Next 1"** Work Seed st to first marker, 23 sts AB Rib, Seed st to end. ****
Next 3 (4, 4)" Work SRS to first marker, 23 sts AB Rib, SRS to end.
Next 1" Repeat from ** to **.
Next 4" Work AB Rib over all sts.
Next row (RS) With L, k33 (36, 39); with B, work 35-st Tube; with L, k to end.
Next 7" Beginning with WS row, work Seed st over all sts.
Next 2 rows Bind off loosely 40 (42, 44) sts at beginning of row, work Seed st to end.
Bind off remaining sts.

Yarns

L natural linen

B black wool

Stitches

Stockinette

Seed

SRS

AB Rib

Tube

LOOSE FIT

Skill Intermediate
Fit Loose
Size S (M, L)
Approximate measurements
A 42 (46, 50)"
B 40 (41, 41)"
C 28 (29, 30)"
Gauge 18 sts and 22 rows to 10cm/4" over Seed st
Yarn Medium weight
L 1380 (1510, 1630) yds linen blend
B 85 yds wool
Needles 5mm/US8, or size to obtain gauge
Extras Faux Fur: 20" × 4" (for collar) and strip of 1" × 2 yds, five ¾" buttons, markers, black sewing thread

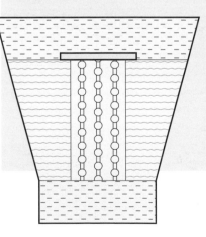

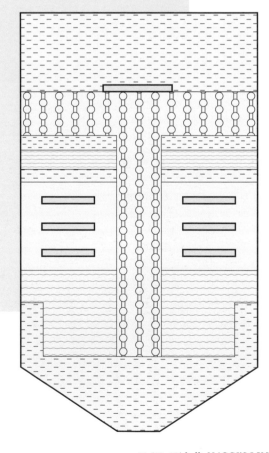

11 (12, 13) balls MAGGI'S LINEN (L) in Natural, 1 ball MAGGI'S MERINO ARAN in Black (B)

LEFT FRONT

With L, cast on 10 sts.
Work Seed st, increasing 1 st at side edge every row (beginning of RS rows and end of WS rows) to 52 (54, 58) sts.
Work 1" even.

Begin border Keeping 10 sts at center Front in Seed st in L (at end of RS rows, at beginning of WS rows: place marker) work remaining sts in patterns and yarns as follows (unless told to work ALL STS):

Next row (RS) Work 10 sts Seed st, 32 (34, 38) sts SRS. Work pattern for 5".

Next 2 (3, 3)" Work AB Rib.

* Next 2" With L, work St st.

Next row (RS) With L, k11; with B, work 20-st Tube; with L, k to end. Repeat from * twice.

All sts, next row (WS) With L, cable cast on 6 sts at beginning of row; work Seed st to marker (16-st border); work St st to end—58 (60, 64) sts.

Next 2" Work St st.

Next 1" Work Seed st.

Next 3 (4, 4)" Work SRS.

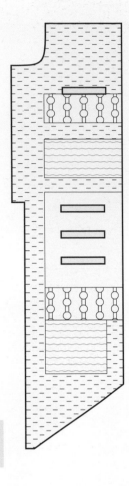

Next 1" Work Seed st.

Next 4" Work AB Rib.

Next row (RS) With L, work 11 sts Seed st; with B, work 20-st Tube; with L, k tube sts, work Seed st to marker.

Next 4" With L, work Seed st, ending with a RS row.

Next row (WS) Bind off 14 (14, 16) sts, work Seed st to end. Continue in Seed st, k2tog at beginning of every WS row 4 times—40 (42, 44) sts.
Work even in Seed st until Front length matches Back.
Bind off loosely.
Mark Front edge for 5 buttons, one at neck, another 1" above 6-st cast-on, and 3 spaced evenly between.

RIGHT FRONT

Work as Left Front, reversing shaping and pattern placement, and on RS rows, matching each button marker on Left Front, work a buttonhole as follows: work 3 sts Seed st, yo, k2tog, work Seed st to marker, work pattern to end.

MAKING UP

Sew shoulder seams. Sew Sleeves to body, centering Sleeve at shoulder seam. Sew side seams leaving 6" open at bottom. Sew Sleeve seams. Fold 2" of Seed st at bottom of Sleeve to inside of Sleeve and stitch lightly. Press seams and edges lightly using a damp cloth. Sew buttons to Left Front edge.

Fur Collar Along sides (4" ends) and top (one 20" side) of Faux Fur piece, turn ½" to wrong side and hem with black sewing thread. Pin unhemmed edge to knitting, fitting evenly around neck, then sew. Weave strips of fur at top of Seed st at cuffs and at top of sleeve, weaving under 1" and over 1". Sew on WS to secure ends of fur. Fluff fur, but DO NOT PRESS FAUX FUR.

Shoulder pads are recommended.

ENNISKERRY TOP

Stitches

 Stockinette

Seed

 Ladder

VERY CLOSE FIT

Skill Intermediate

Fit Very close

Size S (M, L)

Approximate measurements

A 33 (35, 37)"

B 12½ (13½, 13½)" at sides

C 20"

Gauge 16 sts and 20 rows to 10cm/4" over St st with 2 rows L, 2 rows Rag Mix

Yarn Medium weight

L 490 (600, 740) yds linen blend

RY 60 yds rag yarn

S 60 yds slub

M 60 yds mohair

G 60 yds gold metallic

C 60 yds rag yarn

R 60 yds ribbon

Optional ¼ yd gold net or fabric

Needles 5.5mm/US9, or size to obtain gauge

Extras 1½ (2, 2) yds 1" elastic, safety pin

STOCKINETTE STITCH
(St st)
RS rows Knit.
WS rows Purl.

SEED STITCH
Row 1 * K1, p1; repeat from *.
Row 2 P the knit sts and k the purl sts.
Repeat Row 2 for Seed st.

LADDER STITCH
Row 1 (RS) Knit, wrapping yarn around the needle 3 times for every stitch (see page 170).
Row 2 Purl into sts, dropping wraps off needle.

NOTES
1 See *It's Easy*, page 1, for hand-knotting Rag Mix and inserting elastic. *2* When knitting with Rag Mix, keep knots to right side (RS). *3* End each pattern-stitch section with a wrong-side (WS) row.

Color sequence for hand-knotting Rag Mix Cut thirty 10" lengths of each yarn (Optional addition: cut gold net or fabric into 10" × ½" lengths.) Cut more strands as needed. Knot strands together in the following order: RY, L, S, M, G, C, R and gold fabric (if using), leaving 1" tails on knots.

SLEEVES
With Rag Mix, cast on 28 (30, 32) sts.
Work Seed st for 6 rows.
* **Next 2 rows** Work Ladder st.
Next 4 rows Work Seed st. *
Repeat from * to * twice more.
Repeat * to * 7 more times, AT SAME TIME, increase 1 st at beginning and end of first of the 4 Seed st rows—42 (44, 46) sts.
Next 2 rows With Rag Mix, work Seed st.
Casing With L, work 6 rows St st. Purl next (RS) row. Work 6 rows St st. Bind off loosely.

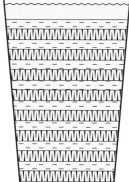

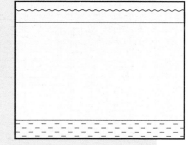

BODY
Back
With L, cast on 66 (70, 74) sts.
Next 1½" Work Seed st, alternating 2 rows L and 2 rows Rag Mix.
Next 10 (11, 11)" Work St st, alternating 2 rows L 2 rows Rag Mix. Work Casing as for Sleeves.
Front
With L, cast on 10 sts in L.
Work Seed st: * 2 rows L, 2 rows Rag Mix; repeat from *, AT SAME TIME, increasing 1 st at beginning and end of every row 20 times—50 sts.
Continuing in pattern, cast on 8 (10, 12) sts at beginning of next 2 rows—66 (70, 74) sts. Work even for 1½".
Next 10 (11, 11)" Work St st: 2 rows L, 2 rows Rag Mix. Work Casing as for Sleeves.

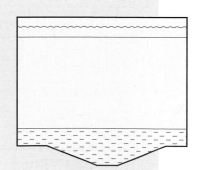

ROSE
With L, cast on 80 sts.
Work Seed st for 3".
Next row * K2tog; repeat from *—40 sts.
Bind off loosely.

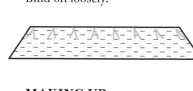

MAKING UP
Sew side seams,
Casing Fold Casing to WS along purl row at top of Body and stitch loosely, leaving an opening for elastic. Measure, cut, and insert elastic. Sew opening closed. Repeat for Sleeves.
Sew top of Sleeve casing to top of Front and Back casings for 3" at side seams.
Gather Rose along bound-off edge and curl into shape. Sew to Front. Optional: At center Back, 3" above bottom, gather center 5" with sewing thread.

4 (5, 6) balls MAGGI'S LINEN (L) in Natural; 1 ball each MAGGI'S MIST SLUB (S) in Beige/red, MAGGI'S MOHAIR (M) in Ivory, MAGGI'S METALLIC (G) in Gold, MAGGI'S RAG in Chocolate (C) and Red (RY) and MAGGI'S RIBBON (R) in Ivory

Yarns

 T *charcoal tweed*

 R *black ribbon*

M *pale grey merino*

Stitches

Stockinette

Seed

SRS

AB Rib

 Basket Weave

Tube

Split

LOOSE FIT

Skill Intermediate

Fit Loose

Size S (M, L)

Approximate measurements

A 40 (44, 48)"

B 25½ (26, 27)"

C 28 (28½, 30)"

Gauge 18 sts and 20 rows to 10cm/4" over St st with T

Yarn Medium weight

T 1070 (1220, 1220) yds wool tweed for sweater, 180 yds for hat

R 195 yds ribbon

M 85 yds wool

Needles 5.5mm/US9 or size to obtain gauge

Optional Faux fur: Two 10" × 5" pieces for cuffs, 22" × 3" for hat, matching thread, stick-on Velcro

STOCKINETTE STITCH (St st)
RS rows Knit.
WS rows Purl.

SEED STITCH
Row 1 * K1, p1; repeat from *.
Row 2 P the knit sts and k the purl sts.
Repeat Row 2 for Seed st.

SINGLE RIDGE STITCH (SRS)
Rows 1 and 3 (RS) Knit.
Rows 2 and 4 (WS) Purl.
Rows 5 and 6 Purl.
Rows 7 and 9 Knit.
Row 8 Purl.
Row 10 Knit.
Repeat Rows 1–10.

ALTERNATING BOBBLE RIB (AB Rib)
Row 1 (RS) * P5, k1; repeat from *.
Rows 2–4 K the knit sts and p the purl sts.
Row 5 P5; * work Bobble (p1, k1, p1, k1) in next st, turn, k4, turn, p4; p5, k1, p5; repeat from *.
Row 6 K the knit sts and p the purl sts, EXCEPT p the 4 Bobble sts together.
Rows 7–10 Repeat Rows 1–4.
Row 11 P5, k1, p5; * work Bobble in next st, p5, k1, p5; repeat from *.
Row 12 Repeat Row 6.
Repeat Rows 1–12.

BASKET WEAVE
Row 1 (RS) * K4, p4; repeat from *.
Rows 2–4 K the knit sts and p the purl sts.
Row 5 * P4, k4; repeat from *.
Rows 6–8 K the knit sts and p the purl sts.
Repeat Rows 1–8.

TUBE
Beginning with a RS row, work 7 rows in St st.
Close Tube Turn work (WS facing): * Slip 1 st from left-hand (LH) needle to right-hand (RH) needle; insert RH needle under strand running between first st and second st on first row of Tube; slip st on RH needle over strand; continue from * across Tube sts. At end of row, slip last st on LH needle to RH needle.

NOTES
1 See *It's Easy*, page 1, for Splits and Tubes. *2* End each pattern-stitch section with a wrong-side (WS) row unless directed to end with a right-side (RS) row. *3* When changing colors, bring new color under old color to prevent holes, and work first row in St st.

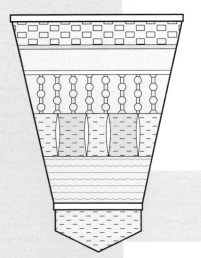

SLEEVES
With T, cast on 4 sts. Work Seed st, increasing 1 st at beginning and end of every row to 32 (34, 34) sts, then work even for 2".
Tube With M, work Tube across all sts.
Increase 1 st at beginning and end of every RS row to 56 sts, then every 3rd row to top of sleeve except Tube rows, AT SAME TIME, work patterns and yarns as follows:
Next 4" With T, work SRS.
3" Seed-st Splits With T, work 14 sts Seed st, turn, work Seed st back and forth on these 14 sts for 3", ending with a RS row (14-st section); with R, work 8-st section; with T, work 4-st section; with R, work 12-st section; with T, work Seed-st section on remaining sts.
Next row (WS) With R, purl.
Next 4" With T, work AB Rib.
Work St st 2 rows M, 1½" T, and 2 rows R.
Next 2" With T, work Basket Weave.
Tube With M, work Tube over all sts.
With T, bind off loosely.

Sweater 7 (8, 8) balls MAGGI'S TWEED FLECK ARAN (T) in Charcoal; 2 balls MAGGI'S RIBBON (R) in Black; 1 ball MAGGI'S MERINO ARAN (M) in Pale Grey
Hat 2 balls MAGGI'S TWEED FLECK ARAN in Charcoal

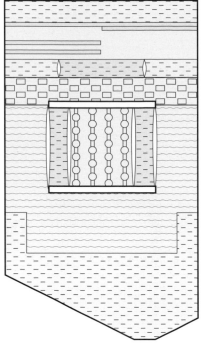

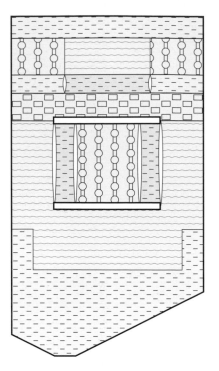

FRONT

With T, cast on 10 sts. Work Seed st, increasing 1 st at beginning and end of every row 15 times—40 sts. Then increase at end of RS rows and beginning of WS rows only 22 (26, 30) times—62 (66, 70) sts. Then increase 1 st at end of RS rows and cable cast on 2 sts at beginning of WS rows 13 (14, 15) times—88 (94, 100) sts.
Work even for 2".
Next 4" Work 10 sts Seed st at beginning and end of rows and SRS on 68 (74, 80) center sts.
Next 3" Work SRS.
7" Splits With T, work 19 (22, 25)-st SRS section, for 7"; with M, work Tube on 50 sts, then, with R, work Seed-st section on first 10 of these 50 sts; with T, work AB-Rib section on next 30 of these 50 sts; with R, work Seed-st section on last 10 of these 50 sts; with T, work SRS section on remaining sts.
Next row (WS) With T, purl.
Next row (RS) With T, k19 (22, 25); with M, work Tube over 50 sts; with T, k Tube sts and to end.
Next row With T, purl.
Next 2 (2½, 3)" Work Basket Weave.
1½" Seed-st Splits With T, work 24 (27, 30)-st Seed-st section for 1½"; with R, work 40-st section; with T, work 24 (27, 30)-st section.
Next row (WS) With T, purl across. **
[**Next row** (RS) With T, k44 (47, 50); with R, k to end. **Next row** Purl T sts with T and R sts with

R. **Next 4 rows** With T, work St st] 2 times.
Next row (RS) With R, k44 (47, 50); with T, k to end.
Next 3 rows Work St st: T sts with T and R sts with R.
Next 2 rows With R, work St st.
Next row (RS) With T, knit.
Next 2" With T, work Seed st. Bind off loosely.

BACK

Work as Front to **, but reverse shaping.
Next 3" Work 25 (28, 31) sts AB Rib, 40 sts SRS, AB Rib to end.
Next 2" With T, work Seed st. Bind off loosely.

OPTIONAL FUR CUFFS
(make 2)

10" × 5" With matching thread, slip-stitch side seam. Turn ½" to wrong side at top and bottom for hem, slip-stitch. Pin or attach with Velcro to cuffs (stick adhesive back of hook side of Velcro to fur). DO NOT PRESS FUR.

MAKING UP

Secure Splits (see page 1) on sleeves. On Front and Back, sew splits closed. Secure ribbon ends with matching thread. Sew shoulder seams, leaving approximately 12" neck opening at center. Center sleeves at shoulder seams and sew sleeves to Front and Back. Sew sleeve seams; sew side seams above Seed st. Press seams lightly using a damp cloth.

HAT

Follow instructions for Peatland Hat (page 115).

Yarns

☐ **T** charcoal tweed

▨ **B** black merino

☐ **M** cream mohair

Stitches

☐ Stockinette

⊡ Seed

▭ Tube

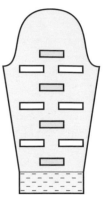

STANDARD FIT

Skill Intermediate

Fit Standard

Size 6 mo (18 mo, 2, 4)

Approximate measurements

A 20½ (22, 23, 25)" Pullover

A 22½ (24, 25, 27)" Cardi, buttoned

B 12 (12, 13½, 14)"

C 17 (18½, 19, 21)"

Gauge 18 sts and 20 rows to 10cm/4" over St st using larger needles and T

Yarn Medium weight

T 300 (450, 450, 610) yds wool tweed

B 85 yds wool

M 110 yds mohair

Needles 5mm/US8 and 5.5mm/US9, or sizes to obtain gauge

Extras Four ¾" buttons for Cardi, elastic thread (option) for Pullover

STOCKINETTE STITCH

(St st)

RS rows Knit.

WS rows Purl.

SEED STITCH

Row 1 * K1, p1; repeat from *.

Row 2 P the knit sts and k the purl sts.

Repeat Row 2 for Seed st.

TUBE

Beginning with a RS row, work 7 rows in St st. (See page 1).

Close Tube Turn work (WS facing): * Slip 1 st from left-hand (LH) needle to right-hand (RH) needle; insert RH needle under strand running between first st and second st on first row of Tube; slip st on RH needle over strand; continue from * across Tube sts. At end of row, slip last st on LH needle to RH needle.

NOTE

End each pattern stitch section with a wrong-side (WS) row, unless directed to end with a right-side (RS) row.

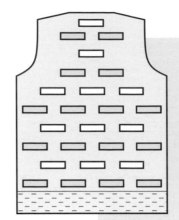

Pullover

BACK

With smaller needles and T, cast on 46 (50, 52, 56) sts. Work Seed st for 10 rows. Change to larger needles and work 2 rows St st.

* **Next row** (RS) With T, k2 (4, 5, 7); [with B, work 6-st Tube; with T, k12] 3 times; with B, work 6-st Tube; with T, k to end.

Next 5 (5, 7, 7) rows With T, work St st, beginning with a WS row.

Next row (RS) With T, k8 (10, 11, 13); [with M, work 6-st Tube; with T, k12] 2 times; with M, work 6-st Tube; with T, k to end.

Next 5 (5, 7, 7) rows With T, work St st, beginning with a WS row.

Repeat from *, AT SAME TIME, at 7 (7, 8, 8)":

Shape armholes Bind off 3 sts at the beginning of next 2 rows—40 (44, 46, 50) sts. Then decrease 1 st at beginning and end of next 5 (6, 6, 7) rows—30 (32, 34, 36) sts. Work even in established pattern until armholes measure 4 (5, 5½, 6)", ending with a WS row.

Bind off 8 (9, 10, 10) sts at beginning of next 2 rows—14 (14, 14, 16) sts. Place remaining sts on holder.

FRONT

Work as Back until armholes measure 1½ (2, 2, 2½)", ending with a WS row.

Shape neck

Next row (RS) Sl1, k10 (10, 11, 11), turn, work back and forth on these 11 (11, 12, 12) sts as follows:

Next row (WS) Sl1, purl to last st, k1.

Next 2 rows Work in pattern, decrease 1 st at neck edge—9 (9, 10, 10) sts.

Work even until armhole measures same as Back, ending with a WS row.

Bind off.

Put center 8 (10, 10, 12) sts on holder and work right side of neck on remaining 11 (11, 12, 12) sts, reversing shaping.

SLEEVES

With smaller needles and T, cast on 24 (26, 26, 26) sts. Work Seed st for 12 rows.

Change to larger needles and work 2 rows St st.

Begin increasing Increase 1 st at beginning and end of 6th and every following 6 (8, 8, 8) th row to 32 (32, 36, 36) sts, then every 4th row to 34 (36, 38, 40) sts, AT

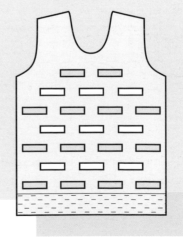

SAME TIME work patterns and yarns as follows:

* **Next row** (RS) With T, k to 6 center sts; with B, work 6-st Tube; with T, k to end. **

Next 5 (5, 7, 7) rows With T, work St st, beginning with a WS row.

Next row (RS) With T, k to center 18 sts; with M, work 6-st Tube; with T, k12; with M, work 6-st Tube; with T, k to end.

Next 5 (5, 7, 7) rows With T, work St st, beginning with a WS row. Repeat from * 2 more times, then from * to ** once.

Shape sleeve cap At beginning of next 14 (16, 14, 18) rows bind off 1 st—20 (20, 24, 22) sts. Work 2 rows even. At beginning of next 4 (4, 6, 4) rows bind off 2 sts—12 (12, 12, 14) sts. Bind off remaining sts.

Sew right shoulder seam.

NECK FRILL

With larger needles and T, with RS facing, and beginning at left shoulder, pick up and k 15 sts along Front neck, k 8 (10, 10, 12) sts from holder, pick up and k 15 sts along right Front neck, k 12 (14, 14, 16) sts of Back neck from holder—50 (54, 54, 58) sts.

Next row (WS) Purl into front and back of every st—100 (108, 108, 116) sts.

Work 9 rows Seed st.

Bind off loosely.

MAKING UP

Sew shoulder and side seams. Sew Sleeve seams. Fit Sleeves into arm-holes and sew. Press lightly using a damp cloth.

Optional Weave doubled elastic thread around neck on WS to keep shape.

Cardi
Back, Fronts, Sleeves and Band
Follow instructions for Inishowen Cardi (page 52), EXCEPT use B and M instead of R and M and bind off Back and Fronts when armholes measure 4 (5, 5½, 6)" and on Front Band work 3 (3, 4, 4)" between buttonholes.

DICKIE BOW

With smaller needles and T, cast on 10 sts. Work Sccd st for 4–5". Bind off.
Wrap yarn around center of bow 7 times to shape and secure. Add elastic or ribbon to fit around neck.

CARDI OR PULLOVER
2 balls MAGGI'S TWEED FLECK ARAN (T) in Charcoal; 1 ball each: MAGGI'S MOHAIR (M) in Ivory, MAGGI'S MERINO ARAN (B) Black

Carrick-a-rede, Gaelic for 'the rock in the road,' refers to the sea road migrating salmon take past this tiny island. The stunning views and breathtaking crossing need no translation.

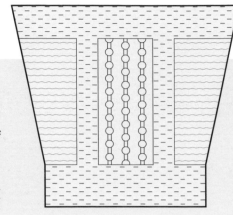

Stitches

 Seed

 SRS

 AB Rib

Short row section

LOOSE FIT

Skill Advanced

Fit Loose

Sizes S (M, L)

Approximate measurements

A 19 (20, 21)" across Front

B 23"

C 28", with cuff turned back

Gauge 16 sts and 20 rows to 10cm/4" over Seed st

Yarn Medium weight

1090 (1100, 1110) yds wool tweed (sweater)

160 yds (hat)

Needles 5.5mm/US9, or size to obtain gauge

Extras Markers, two ¾" buttons

SEED STITCH
Row 1 * K1, p1; repeat from *.
Row 2 P the knit sts and k the purl sts.
Repeat Row 2 for Seed st.

SINGLE RIDGE STITCH (SRS)
Rows 1 and 3 (RS) Knit.
Rows 2 and 4 (WS) Purl.
Rows 5 and 6 Purl.
Rows 7 and 9 Knit.
Row 8 Purl.
Row 10 Knit.
Repeat Rows 1–10.

ALTERNATING BOBBLE RIB (AB Rib)
Row 1 (RS) * P5, k1; repeat from *.
Rows 2–4 K the knit sts and p the purl sts.
Row 5 P5; * work Bobble [(p1, k1, p1, k1) in next st, turn, k4, turn, p4], p5, k1, p5; repeat from *.
Row 6 K the knit sts and p the purl sts, EXCEPT p the 4 Bobble sts together.
Rows 7–10 Repeat Rows 1–4.
Row 11 P5, k1, p5; * work Bobble in next st, p5, k1, p5; repeat from *.
Row 12 Repeat Row 6.
Repeat Rows 1–12.

NOTES
1 See *Techniques*, page 170, for cable cast-on and wrap & turn (W&T) for short rows. *2* End each pattern-stitch section with a wrong-side (WS) row unless directed otherwise.

SLEEVES
Cast on 63 sts.
Work Seed st for 4".
Begin increasing Increase 1 st at beginning and end of every 6th row to top of Sleeve, AT SAME TIME, work patterns as follows:
Next row (RS) Work 12 sts SRS, place marker, work 8 sts Seed st, 23 sts AB Rib, 8 sts Seed st, place marker, work 12 sts SRS. Work pattern for 13 (12, 12)".
Next 3" Work Seed st (adjust length here if necessary).
Bind off loosely.

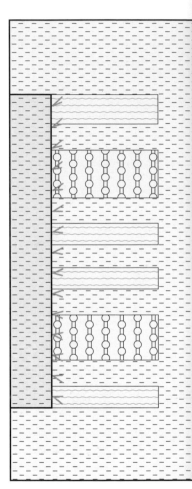

BACK
Note Back is knit from side to side with short-row shaping.
Cast on 66 (70, 74) sts.
Work Seed st for 6 (7, 8)".
Swing Shaping
Short Rows 1, 2: RS row Work 14 sts Seed st, place marker, work 32 (36, 40) sts SRS, turn work (leaving 20 sts unworked). **WS row** Work SRS to marker, Seed st to end.
Short Rows 3, 4: RS row Work Seed st to marker, work 32 (36, 40) sts SRS, wrap next st and turn work (W&T). **WS row** Work SRS to marker, Seed st to end.
Row 5 (RS) Work Seed st to marker, work 32 (36, 40) sts SRS, work 20 sts Seed st.
Row 6 (WS) Work 20 sts Seed st, SRS to marker, Seed st to end.
Repeat Rows 1–6 for 3".
Continue swing shaping [2 rows over 46 (50, 54) sts with no wrap, 2 rows over 46 (50, 54) sts with wrap, 2 rows over all sts] and keep 14-st border and 20 sts worked only on Rows 5 and 6 in Seed st, AT SAME TIME, work patterns on center 32 (36, 40) sts as follows:
* **Next 2"** Work Seed st.
Next 4" Work AB Rib.
Next 2" Work Seed st.
Next 2" Work SRS. **
Next 3" Work Seed st.
Work in reverse from ** to *.
Work 3" SRS.
Next 6 (7, 8)" End swing shaping: Work Seed st over all sts, all rows.
Bind off loosely.

MAGGI'S TWEED FLECK ARAN in
*Black: **Sweater** 8 balls*
***Hat** 2 balls*

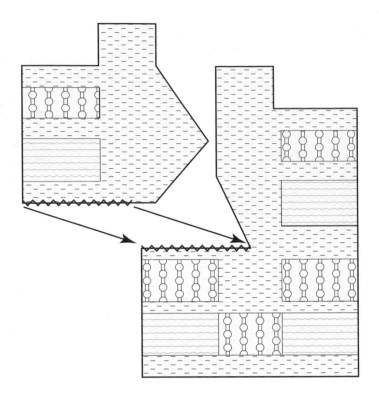

FRONT

Cast on 77 (81, 85) sts.
Work Seed st for 2".
Next 4" Work 26 (28, 30) sts SRS, 25 sts AB Rib, 26 (28, 30) sts SRS.
Next 4 rows Work Seed st.
Next 4" Work 26 (28, 30) sts AB Rib, 25 sts Seed st, 26 (28, 30) sts AB Rib.
Next 4 rows Work Seed st, increasing 1 st at beginning and end of first row—79 (83, 87) sts.
Divide for neck, Left Front,
Next row (RS) Work 40 (42, 44) sts Seed st. Turn and work back and forth on these sts for 5 more rows, placing remaining 39 (41, 43) sts on holder for Right Front.
Next row (RS) Work 26 (28, 30) sts SRS, place marker, work 14 sts Seed st. Work pattern for 4", AT SAME TIME, increase 1 st at center Front (at end of RS row) every 4th row to 50 (52, 54) sts.
Next 6 rows Work Seed st.
Next row (RS) Work 26 (28, 30) sts AB Rib, work remaining sts Seed st. Work pattern for 3".
Next 2" Work Seed st.
Next row (RS) Bind off 26 (29, 31) sts and work remaining 24 (23, 23) sts Seed st for 3" (back collar extension).
Bind off.

Right Front

Next row (RS) Cable cast on 15 sts and continue Seed st on these 15 sts and 39 (41, 43) sts from holder—54 (56, 58) sts.

Next 5 rows Work Seed st, working a buttonhole on next to last (RS) row (work 4 sts Seed st, yarn over, k2tog, work Seed st to end).
Next row (RS) Work 28 sts Seed st, place marker, work 26 (28, 30) sts SRS. Work pattern for 4", AT SAME TIME, increase 1 st at center Front (at beginning of RS row) every other row and work a buttonhole 2" above first buttonhole.
Next 6 rows Continue increasing, and work all sts Seed st.
Next row (RS) K2tog, work Seed st to marker, work 26 (28, 30) sts AB Rib. Work pattern for 3", AT SAME TIME, k2tog at beginning of every RS row until 50 (52, 54) sts remain.
Next 2" Work Seed st, ending with a RS row.
Next row (WS) Bind off 26 (29, 31) sts and work remaining 24 (23, 23) sts Seed st for 3".
Bind off.

TIES (make 2)

Cast on 20 sts.
Work Seed st for 20".
Bind off.

MAKING UP

Sew collar extension bind-offs together. Sew shoulder seams. Sew collar extension to center of Back. Sew Sleeves to body, centering Sleeve at shoulder seam. Sew Ties to Front at bottom sides. Sew side seams above Ties. Sew Sleeve seams.
Press seams lightly using a damp cloth. Sew buttons on Left Front, matching buttonholes. Turn down collar and press lightly. Turn back 2" cuffs and press.

Shoulder pads are recommended.

HAT

Follow instructions for Peatland Hat (page 115).

The sea still pounds where these proud towers once witnessed the humbling of the Spanish Armada— the North coast of Ireland.

A lovely cage perched at the very edge of the sea.

ARDEE SHELL

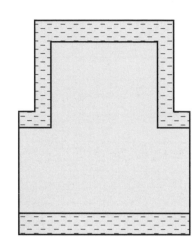

NOTES
1 Use 2 strands held together throughout. *2* End each pattern-stitch section with a wrong-side (WS) row.

FRONT AND BACK
Cast on 50 (54, 58) sts.
Work Seed st for 2".
Next 2" Work St st.
* Next row (RS) K7 (9, 11) sts, [p1, k11] across to last 7 (9, 11) sts, k to end.
Next 2" Work St st.
Next row (RS) K1 (3, 5) sts, [p1, k11] across to last 1 (3, 5) sts, k to end.
Next 2" Work St st.
Repeat from * until piece measures 10 (11, 11)" from cast-on.
Next 1½" Work 12 sts Seed st, place marker, 26 (30, 36) sts in pattern, place marker, 12 sts Seed st.
Next 2 rows Bind off 7 (8, 8) sts, work in pattern to end of row—36 (38, 42) sts.

STOCKINETTE STITCH
(St st)
RS rows Knit.
WS rows Purl.

SEED STITCH
Row 1 * K1, p1; repeat from *.
Row 2 P the knit sts and k the purl sts.
Repeat Row 2 for Seed st.

Next 5" Work 5 sts Seed st, 26 (28, 32) sts in pattern, 5 sts Seed st.
Next 1½ (2, 2)" Work Seed st. Bind off loosely.

MAKING UP
Sew side seams. Sew 1" shoulder seams. Press seams lightly using a damp cloth.

Stitches

 Stockinette

 Seed

B | A

VERY CLOSE FIT

Skill Easy
Fit Very Close
Size S (M, L)
Approximate Measurements
A 31 (33½, 36)"
B 19 (20, 20)"
Gauge 13 sts and 17 rows to 10cm/4" over St st using 2 strands of L
Yarn Medium weight
650 (725, 800) yds linen blend
Needles 6.5mm/US10½, or size to obtain gauge
Extras Markers

6 (6, 7) balls MAGGI'S LINEN in Black

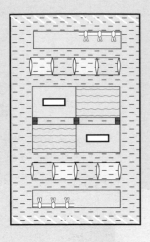

Yarns

	L black linen
	W white linen
	R white ribbon
	RY white rag knot yarn

Stitches

	Stockinette
	Seed
	SRS
	Whip
	Tube
	Split

Skill Intermediate
Approximate measurements 16" × 12"
Gauge 18 sts and 24 rows to 10cm/4"
over Seed st with L
Yarn Medium weight
For 6 mats
L 1000 yds linen blend
W 125 yds linen blend
R 95 yds ribbon
RY 65 yds rag yarn or ½ yd black/white
gingham
Needles 5mm/US8, or size to obtain
gauge
Extras Markers, sewing thread

STOCKINETTE STITCH
(St st)
RS rows Knit.
WS rows Purl.

SEED STITCH
Row 1 * K1, p1; repeat from *.
Row 2 P the knit sts and k the purl sts.
Repeat Row 2 for Seed st.

SINGLE RIDGE STITCH (SRS)
Rows 1 and 3 (RS) Knit.
Rows 2 and 4 (WS) Purl.
Rows 5 and 6 Purl.
Rows 7 and 9 Knit.
Row 8 Purl.
Row 10 Knit.
Repeat Rows 1–10.

TUBE
Beginning with a RS row, work 7 rows in St st.
Close Tube Turn work (WS facing): * Slip 1
st from left-hand (LH) needle to right-hand
(RH) needle; insert RH needle under strand
running between first st and second st on first
row of Tube; slip st on RH needle over strand;
continue from * across Tube sts. At end of row,
slip last st on LH needle to RH needle.

NOTES
1 See It's Easy, page 1, for Splits and Tubes.
2 End each pattern-stitch section with a
wrong-side (WS) row, unless directed to end
with a right-side (RS) row. *3* When changing colors, bring new color under old color
to prevent holes, and work first row in St st.
4 Cut rag yarn into 8" lengths (or gingham
into 10" × ½" lengths) and knot together,
leaving 1" tails.

TABLEMAT
With L, cast on 60 sts.
Work Seed st for 1½".
Begin borders Keeping 10 sts at beginning
and end of every row in Seed st with L (place
markers), work center 40 sts in patterns and
yarns as follows (unless directed to work
ALL STS):
Next row (RS) With L, k20; with RY, p20,
keeping knots to RS.
Next row (WS) With L, k20, p20.
Next 4 rows With L, work St st.
Next 4 rows With L, work Seed st.
* **All sts, 1½" Seed-st Splits** (RS) With L,
work 10 sts Seed st, turn, work back and
forth in Seed st for 1½", ending with a RS
row (10-st section); work 10-st sections in R,
L, R, L, L.
Next row (WS) With L, purl.
Next 4 rows Work Seed st. *
** **Next row** (RS) Work 20 sts St st, 20 sts
SRS. Work pattern for 9 more rows.
Next row (RS) With L, k5; with W, work
10-st Tube; with L, k15 (Tube sts and next 5
sts), work 20 sts SRS.
Next row (WS) With L, work 20 sts SRS, 20
sts St st. Work pattern for 10 more rows.
Next 6 rows Work Seed st.
Repeat from **, EXCEPT reverse placement
of SRS and St st.
Repeat from* to *, EXCEPT work yarns for
Splits as follows: L, L, R, L, R, L.
Next 4 rows Work St st.
Next row (RS) With RY, p20; with L, k20.
Next row (WS) With L, p20, k20.
Next 1½" Work Seed st.
Bind off loosely.

MAKING UP
Secure Splits (page 1). Secure ribbon ends
with matching thread. Press lightly using a
damp cloth.
Using 2 strands of W, whip stitch at ends of
mat, stitching 1" apart and 1" deep.
Using contrast yarn (red shown), make 3
long sts on center row.

For 6 mats 8 balls MAGGI'S LINEN (L)
in Black; 1 ball each: MAGGI'S LINEN
in White (W), MAGGI'S RIBBON (R) in
White, MAGGI'S RAG (RY) in White

My passion for food was born in my family's kitchen. In all Irish families, the credit for cooking goes to Mother and Grandmother. With their guidance I learned the fundamentals of food preparation and the traditions of Irish fare. While the other kids in school had peanut butter sandwiches for lunch, I would open my lunch box to find a hearty sandwich of cured ham drenched with the rich juices of homegrown tomatoes, accompanied by a fresh wheaten scone spilling with my Gran's tasty rhubarb jam. I gained a sincere appreciation for good eating, and I never swapped lunches with anyone!

Eventually, the hunger for a broader culinary education took me to the Northern Ireland Hotel and Catering College, where I earned four Qualifications while building my experience working part-time in local establishments. Afterward, culinary opportunities awaited me on Cape Cod, Massachusetts, home of many wonderful seafood restaurants. The experience I gained there gave me the confidence to enter the Culinary Arts Degree Programme at the University of Ulster. Although I'm nearing the completion of my degree, the world of cooking will continue to challenge and inspire me. At Catering College I met Maggie's daughter Kerrie and that is how I came to be part of this book. Our son Jake had to get in on the act as well, as the youngest model in the book. These dishes represent Irish sustenance using traditional ingredients and reflect the colors and textures of Maggie's place settings. I hope you enjoy the recipes and the unusual locations Alexis had us display them in as much as I did. I welcome your comments or questions.

—*Chef Stevie*
Chef_stephen@hotmail.com

Oysters are farmed in various locations around Ireland, but the warm bays on the East coast offer ideal conditions for producing some of the best oysters in the world. Considered a delicacy by the first Viking settlers, the tasty shellfish were eventually farmed and sold to wealthy landowners. Nearly two hundred years of farming produced successful techniques that are still in use today.

Traditionally served raw or in a stew with other shellfish (boiled in a cauldron over an open fire), oysters are a versatile food product. Modern cooks enjoy a wide array of recipes for this gift of the sea.

Appetizer
EAST COAST OYSTERS
Serves Two

2 Native Oysters
4–5 leaves of Curly Endive (Chicory) Hearts
⅓ cup Honey
⅔ cup Olive Oil
6 pinches Cayenne Pepper
¼ cup Flour

1. Shuck the oysters, remove and retain the flesh.
2. Wash the shells inside and out; they will be used for presentation.
3. Prepare a dressing by mixing the honey with approximately 3 tablespoons olive oil. Set aside.
4. Stir the cayenne pepper into the flour and coat the oysters with the flour/pepper mix.
5. Fry the floured oysters in a hot pan with the remainder of the olive oil—10 seconds on all sides is sufficient.
6. Dress the endive leaves with the honey dressing and place them in the clean oyster shells.
7. Place the fried oysters on the bed of endive and top with dressing, and serve.

In Irish history sustenance depended as much on woodland harvesting as it did on the cultivation of field crops. The vast woodlands supplied the locals with wild apples, berries, and many edible plants and herbs. Traditional Irish cooking used every product available. From the milk of the native cattle, goats, and sheep, cheese was made in the home. Then, as now, cheese and freshly baked breads were an important accompaniment for stews and broths. Cashel Blue Cheese, Ireland's most famous cheese, takes its name from the ancient Rock of Cashel, which overlooks the Tipperary Plains. Here is a recipe that combines this Irish treat with fresh ingredients of the land.

Soup
BERRY & CASHEL BLUE CHEESE SOUP
Serves Two

1 cup peeled and diced Apples
1 cup diced Potatoes
½ cup diced White Onion
1 cup diced Cashel Blue Cheese
2 cups Chicken Stock
2 pinches ground Coriander
1 pinch Fine Sea Salt
1 pinch ground White Peppercorns
1 small cube Unsalted Butter
1 cup Blueberries
1 squeeze Lemon Juice

1. Melt the butter in a large saucepan. Add the potatoes and onion, saute for 5 to 10 minutes until soft.
2. Add the apples, chicken stock, ground cilantro, and lemon juice to the pan. Bring the mixture to the boil, then lower the heat; cover and simmer for 10 to 15 minutes.
3. Add ¾ of the berries and cook for 5 minutes more, or until the potatoes are cooked through.
4. Put half the stew into a blender or food processor. Add ¾ of the cheese and puree.
5. Fold the puree into the remaining soup. Season with salt and pepper.
6. Garnish the dish with the remaining berries and diced cheese.

Fish has always been a staple of the Irish diet, and as a result, the Emerald Isle's history and mythology are rich with fishing lore. Salmon was the most prized of all fish and was considered a source of magical powers. In the olden days, to wish a person 'the health of the salmon' was to bestow blessings of wisdom, strength, and good fortune. Colcannon, a traditional dish of potatoes and cabbage, has been consumed since the introduction of the potato into Ireland in the 16th century and is still popular in modern Irish cuisine. Wild garlic was once abundant in the Irish woodlands. During Lent, feasts were held in honor of wild garlic, which was believed to have medicinal powers to cleanse the body and the spirit. With the broad availability of the French and Italian cultivars, the use of wild garlic has faded from modern cooking, but the plant can still be found in the countryside. We discovered it growing wild at the Mussenden Temple.

Fish course
WILD ATLANTIC SALMON WITH COLCANNON, CRISPY SEAWEED & WILD GARLIC
Serves Two

2 Fillets of Wild Atlantic Salmon
2 Large Potatoes, peeled and quartered
½ Small Spring Cabbage, shredded
3 Spring Onions, chopped
1 pinch Fresh Grated Nutmeg
1 pinch Sea Salt
1 pinch Pepper
3–4 cubes Butter
½ cup Olive Oil
¼ cup Flour
½ cup Milk
½ cup Apple Juice
Wild Garlic Leaves, washed and stemmed
Fresh Seaweed

Colcannon
1. Boil the potatoes.
2. While potatoes are cooking, fry the cabbage, half of the wild garlic, and spring onions in butter to soften.
3. Drain and mash the potatoes with salt, pepper, milk, and apple juice. Add cabbage mixture to the mashed potatoes and grate in the fresh nutmeg.

Salmon
1. Trim the salmon fillets and season with pepper. Cook for 5 minutes on each side in a hot pan with oil and butter.
2. Slice the seaweed, shake off any excess moisture, coat with flour, and deep fry in cooking oil until crisp. Drain and sprinkle with a little salt.

To Present
Place a seared salmon fillet atop a bed of colcannon. Garnish with seaweed and wild garlic leaves. Drizzle with a touch of olive oil.

W ild game birds were hunted and prepared for special meals on religious and festive holidays. Feathered game was traditionally cooked by covering the bird in clay and baking it in a hot fire. When the clay was baked hard, the bird was removed from the fire and cracked open; the feathers and skin came away with the clay to reveal moist, nutrient-rich meat. While this recipe uses modern conveniences, another Irish tradition—Guinness stout—is included as the basis of the sauce. And of course, you can drink what isn't used!

Main course

WILD FOWL, ROOT VEGETABLES & A GUINNESS GAME REDUCTION

Serves Two

1 Fresh Wild Fowl
1 Large Carrot
1 Large Parsnip
¼ Small Turnip
¼ Small Celeriac Root
¼ cup Guinness Stout
½ cup Double Cream
4 sprigs Fresh Rosemary
1 tablespoon fresh Thyme, chopped
1 tablespoon fresh Sage, chopped
1 pinch Salt
1 pinch ground Black Pepper

1. Remove the fowl's breast and reserve the rest of the bird for the stock.
2. Top, tail and peel the root vegetables, retain the scraps.
3. Boil, then puree each vegetable separately. Store in separate bowls.
4. Place reserved bird on a roasting tray and brown in the oven at 400°F for 30 minutes.
5. Add the vegetable scraps and roast for 5 minutes more.
6. Transfer the roasted bird and vegetable scraps to a pot and add water to cover. Bring to a boil, then reduce heat and simmer until 2–3 inches of stock remains at the bottom of the pot. Strain the stock through a fine sieve; discard the solids.
7. Remove the tender fillets from the underside of the breasts, discarding any tendons or skin, and combine with any meat left on the carcass.
8. Place the meat in a blender or food processor, and pulse the blades to form a pulp. Add the cream, salt, pepper, thyme, and sage and blend to form a mousseline.
9. Pierce a hole through the breast from bone to tip. Fill a piping bag with the mousseline, and pipe it into the breast.
10. Seal the breast's skin by searing it in a hot pan, then roast at 350°F for 8 to 12 minutes.
11. Meanwhile, bring the stock to the boil, then simmer to reduce it to a glaze. Add the Guinness and reduce by one-third.
12. Warm the vegetable purees and layer them on the plate, alternating colors.
13. Slice the breast diagonally and arrange on top of the vegetables.
14. Glaze and top with rosemary sprigs.

Cottage cheese gets its name from its traditional production in the home. Easy to make, its popularity throughout Ireland was aided by its nutritional value and versatility. All over Ireland hedge-row fruits are widely available, from blackberries, raspberries, wild strawberries to gooseberries, sloes, and blueberries. They served as desserts or treats in olden times, providing essential natural sugars. In this dish I have combined the two to create a dessert that balances the acidity and sweetness from the wild fruits with the mellow creaminess of the cottage cheese—a complimentary end to an Irish meal.

Dessert
COTTAGE CHEESE WITH WOODLAND FRUITS
Serves Two

1½ cups Cottage Cheese
3 ounces Mascarpone Cheese
2 tablespoons Sugar
20 Blackberries
20 Blueberries
10 Raspberries

1 cup Balsamic Vinegar
¼ cup Brown Sugar
1½ tablespoons Vintage Port
Chocolate
Rose Petals

1. Mix together the cottage cheese, mascarpone cheese, and sugar until the sugar has dissolved. Refrigerate for one hour.
2. Place the balsamic vinegar, raspberries, half the blackberries, and half the blueberries in a pan with the brown sugar and the port. Bring to a boil, then reduce heat and simmer until a thick syrup is formed. Strain out the fruit and allow to cool.

To present
Layer the chilled cheese mix with the remaining fruit and drizzle with the reduced balsamic syrup. Decorate with chocolate and rose petals.

Our XRX crew celebrates the sun at the beach in Cushendun—(clockwise from left) Stylist Rick Mondragon; Book Editor Elaine Rowley; Photographer Alexis Xenakis; Photo Assistants David Xenakis and Karen Bright; Author Maggie Jackson; and Model Shannon Brown.

COLOPHON
On location in Maggie's Ireland

Don't let this map of *Maggie's Ireland* fool you—the sun is a figment of artist Natalie Sorenson's imagination, pure artistic license. May, the month Maggie Jackson said would be the driest, turned out to be the wettest. Not in a decade, not in a century—but in Irish history!

Days would go by with Ireland beckoning and with our crew rained in, passing the time in picturesque seaside cottages. Then, for a short while, the rain would stop. Filtered by the clouds, the muted light would create unforgettable images of the Emerald Isle. Then the rain would start again, and it was time to seek cover.

1 We were so lucky to find Mussenden Temple open. This rotunda, built on the very edge of the Antrim Coast by the Bishop of Derry in 1785, provided us with shelter—and panoramic views. *2* Our cover model, Nuala Meenehan, drenched but still smiling. *3* Bishop's Gate (where Chef Stevie got wild garlic leaves for our food shots) leads to Mussenden Temple. *4* Finn McCool, legendary Giant, heading to Scotland via the Giant's Causeway which, legend says, he built so he could visit his lady love across the water. Naturally he'll be presenting her with some greenery—and one of Maggie's jackets. *5* Carrick-a-rede Rope Bridge—a magnificent National Trust site, connects the North of Ireland with a tiny island *(6)*. We'll never forget Nuala swaying on it—in high heels, in a gale. *7* Rathlin Island—and puffins!—were only a short boat-ride away, but the rain kept falling. *8* Umbrellas, umbrellas, and more umbrellas. *9* Rick, steaming up a storm. *10* A modeling debut. *11* Who needs maps? *12* Rained-out again at Cushendun? No problem—Photo Assistant Karen Bright has some finishing to do for Maggie. *13* Queen Victoria, in front of Belfast City Hall, clad in Maggie finery. *14* 'Big Fish' at Belfast's Laganside. *15* Belfast's Queen's University. *16* Another gazebo, another shelter. *17* Linen guard tower and *(18)* small cottage at Ulster Folk and Transport Museum. *19* Temple of the Winds replica, lyre topiary *(20)*, and swans *(21)* at Mount Stewart. *22* Photo Assistant David Xenakis taking his shots. *23* Magnificent Greyabbey. *24* Park Cottage. *25* A Pavlova for a birthday boy. *26* The Slieve Donard Hotel in Newcastle became our refuge in a storm. *27* Half-timbered house along the road. *28* Silent Valley hidden in the Mourne Mountains. *29* Field walls showcase Maggie's knits. *30* Maggie warm and cozy at 'Rosie's Cottage.' *31* Posing. *32* Elaine and a Victorian love seat—for the XRX Mascots. *33* Flax stooks. *34* Eugene McConville and *(35)* his scutching mill. *36* Rain, rain, go away! *37* Alexis perched on the Grianán of Aligh. *38* Warning sign. *39* Time to pack up. *40* Pagan idol on eerie Boa Island. *41* Silent faces on White Island. *42* Captain Mickey, his dog, and Big Red on Lower Lough Erne. *43* Round tower at Devenish Island. *44* Putting a passerby to good use. *45* Wish you were here! *46* Journey's end.

COLOPHON
Maggie's Ireland: land of mist, legend—and linen

(Counterclockwise, from top)
Eugene McConville, his flax field, his water wheel, his scutched flax—keeping an old tradition alive; baby pigs having their 'tea;' a story-book thatched cottage on the road to Enniskillen; stone faces at dusk at White Island.

The man with a dark jacket, herringbone hat, Aran sweater, reddish cheeks, and weathered hands kneels at a small plot beside his home. He pulls a clump of green out of the ground, holds it up for his visitors, and says, "This is flax."

These tiny plants fill the small field bordered on one side by his yard and on the other by a small stream. "This is a diversion channel of the River Lagan," he says, "which rises in the famous Mourne Mountains, flows through Dromore, and down to Belfast Lough. The river provided the energy for the mills that scutched, separated the wooden fiber from the flax, in this area.

"I was reared with flax—in my family it goes back to the middle of the 1850s, to my grandmother's time. We've been working at flax ever since. Once, twelve, fourteen, sixteen tons of flax went through this mill a week. But the flax industry no longer exists here—I'm doing this to keep an old craft alive."

It's a rainy Monday morning as Eugene McConville bids us to follow him. He walks toward the sound of water, the mill whose roof, and some of its walls, are made of metal corrugated sheets that used to be bright red, but are now covered with the pale green of lichens and algae.

Eugene opens the mill's black wooden door and raises the sluice gate. As the water rushes through, the mill turns into a cataract. "When I was about five years old…" Eugene shouts, but it's hard to hear him over the sound of rushing water. The sluice gate has unleashed not just a flood of the River Lagan but of memories as well. "I remember my father saying, 'Eugene, don't go too near the water. That's a big water wheel driving the machinery. Watch those flat belts, those cog wheels. Too dangerous for little boys.' But I couldn't stay away from it then, or now—isn't it beautiful?"

As if nudged awake from a deep sleep, the giant wheel creaks. And, very, very slowly at first, it begins to turn. What a moment ago had been rusting and immobile has turned into a mesmerizing circle whose hypnotic revolutions bring back memories of another little boy, and another stream.

His mother, and other village women, are trekking down the steep mountainside, leading their horses laden with bundles of flax.

Annoying my happiness…

It rained some more, we drove; it poured, and we drove on—Alexis was going to White Island to see those statues, by hook or by crook. The island was only a short distance from the Lough Erne shores, but was there a human in sight, a boat, or any life at all? We had traveled, squashed in our van, for miles and miles to find that the Lemy (the ferry) only sails at weekends and the other boats were in for the day.

Of course, we didn't arrive until 4:30 p.m. At the national park, a lonely figure appeared (quite handsome, in fact) out of the heavy rain and mist, and I explained we were desperate, as we could not return. After saying we had no chance of getting to the island except to swim (not so good for Alexis' cameras), as a last resort he gave us a number to ring.

So, although he had just finished for the day and was about to have his tea, a kind fisherman offered to take us out to the island. However, I took one look at the boat and the rough waves on the lake and decided I was staying in the van! Rick and Karen agreed. About an hour and a half later, a very excited and wet threesome returned with lots more photos. I will let them tell that story!

On the way there, we passed a fabulous thatched house outside Enniskillen, sitting amidst a small forest of trees. The sign said, 'Trespassers Prosecuted,' but of course when it suits him, Alexis only understands Greek.

Everywhere we went, bad weather followed. At the Ulster Folk and Transport Museum Coshkib Hill farm the sun shone for a while—then the hailstones came and they got bigger and bigger. It gave us time to look at the newborn pigs. The hens didn't mind us either.

There was an old man dressed in clothes like farmers wore many years ago. His trousers were tied up with bailer twine; I remember my Grandpa Fyffe doing the same, and, of course, with a pipe in his mouth as well.

Stopping briefly at my mum's house brought to mind one of my stories of being a young designer and using poppies to create fashion (see page 164).

My mum, a very, very special person, still lives at the house where I grew up—and where flowers are now safer!

(Clockwise from above)
Captain Mickey and Big Red took us to White Island; Captain Mickey's dog (posing as a photographer's assistant); XRX at Boa Island; poppies bloom without fear of becoming fashion; Maggie's mum's garden; Romanesque ruins at White Island; journey's end.

Maggie and her mother, Sylvia—a beautiful country, a loving family, and a dream.

(From bottom)
Maggie's grandson Jake between shots;
ruins of 12th-century Greyabbey on the
Strangford Lough; guard tower overlooking
the linen-bleaching field.

They submerge the flax sheaves in the shallow river, and they put stones over them to keep the flax in place. After about a week, the flax is brought to the village and spread out to dry. Then the flax breaks, mimicking giant cicadas, fill the afternoons with their incessant chatter...

The sound of Eugene's voice breaks in, and once again I'm surrounded by the thundering wheel turning at top speed. "I'm so proud of this wheel," Eugene says. "About 70 tons of water a minute, over a ton a second, yes sir," Eugene says. "It is 2 meters wide, 6 meters deep, has 42 buckets, and it's over 100 years of age."

All those metal cogs and long leather belts transfer the water's power to a long steel shaft—the scutching stations—that gives this mill its name. "Blades made of beech," Eugene says, "spin around at high speed and the scutcher, as he's called, holds the flax on this little stand. The wooden blades are coming around, lashing the waste out, leaving the flax fiber ready to be spun.

"The scutchers were mostly men, but some women would have worked at the breakers. That's another machine, a half-way stage, that the flax passes through before scutching, softening the core."

He picks up a sheaf of flax from a nearby table and holds it close to a narrow opening in the wooden partition. Fast-moving blades, like tiny propellers, whirl by in a blur. And, as if by magic, with waste fiber flying everywhere, the narrow, dry, cylindrical flax stalks reveal their treasure.

"Normally, three-quarters of the flax would be waste, one-quarter saleable fiber," Eugene says. Well, not total waste: in the old days the waste could be used in the open hearth to heat the house.

"And there are quite a few grades of flax," Eugene says. "Number one would be perfection: unbroken for about a meter, almost impossible to get.

"The public lorry came to our mill to take our flax to market. It was during the last war, fuel was on the ration, and there were no private lorries. Maybe six, seven, eight tons going to market on a Monday and also the same on Thursday. So there was quite a lot of flax going out of this small mill. And the farmer would have been there to see his flax graded and sold. Then it would be taken to the spinning mill to be spun into

yarn or the weaving mill to become linen fabric. You didn't have very much linen when I was young; you wouldn't have used it extravagantly.

"Did you see the open tanks out back? We had machinery that would set the bales down, to ret the flax. 'Ret' means 'halfway to rot,' to loosen the fiber from its wooden core. We'd steep the flax for about ten nights, then it would be taken out into the field. In about three days a turner came along, turning the flax over. And in another three days—depending on the weather—the round baler came along, baled the flax, and brought it to the scutching mill.

"This was very much a working mill up to 1955, one of 32 mills in County Down alone. There were more in County Antrim, and lots more in County Tyrone... At one time we had over 50 workers, but now it's just a working museum.

"There were lots of mills operating here in the north—and lots of farmers growing flax. A farmer would bring anywhere from 2,000–10,000 'beets' to the mill. These bundles weighed about ten pounds each and there would be 700 or 800 beets from one acre. Small farmers would grow two, three acres; for large farmers, 30 acres was common.

"In those days we didn't have modern machinery; if you grew a lot of flax, it meant a lot of work: the flax was pulled by hand. You'd pull a sheaf, make a band with a few stalks, put it down. Sheaves were gathered into beets, and 12 beets made a 'stook.' A sheaf of flax was about two inches in diameter, so it was a good day's pulling, that much flax. The farmers brought in pullers, so the more they pulled, the better for themselves.

"They could have pulled 20 stooks in a day. That would have been considered a good day's pulling. It was back-breaking work, starting maybe 5 or 6 o'clock on a good summer morning at the end of July and August, even up to September. They would have worked up to 9 and 10 at night, and they would have had 20 stooks. Some hard workers who wanted to make more money could have pulled up to 30 stooks. That's 30 multiplied by 12—a lot of pulling in a day.

"The pullers pulled, and the farmers hauled the flax down to the lint pond with their horses and carts. Stones were put on top of the flax, after ten nights in the water they took the stones off, and carted the flax out to the fields to dry. Then, in about two or three days, it was gathered into racks to let the wind and the sun dry it out. The weather had a big say in the matter."

Ah, the weather. This was our third visit to Dromore, just south of Lisburn, about an hour from Belfast, to see Eugene and photograph his scutch mill. And the third time we were rained out. Harsh flash lighting just wouldn't do for natural linen, so there was nothing to do but wait for the clouds to part long enough to let a few rays of sunshine through. As Eugene continues with his story, a light rain is still tap-dancing on the mill's tin roof. Now you know why those red panels—and Ireland—are so green.

Just before 7 p.m., the rain stops, the sun peers through the clouds, Eugene proudly holds his newly scutched linen—and we have our picture. Then Eugene lowers the sluice gate and shuts the mill door, but not before catching his new linen on its top edge, allowing it to wave in the wind.

"We would sow flax at the end of March up to the end of April," he says. "After about 14 weeks it's ready for harvesting. But after the last war the cry was to produce food. The farmers, each year, were growing less and less flax, had more potatoes, oats, pigs, and cattle on their land. As the flax decreased, my father, who was also a dairy farmer, increased our herd. We were able to adjust, but I miss that time, I have such wonderful memories. By the late 1950s and early '60s the flax industry had moved

(From top, left to right)

The Percy French Restaurant at Newcastle provided shelter—and food; mist clouds the Silent Valley in the Mourne Mountains; a Slieve Donard gazebo becomes a giant umbrella; finishing touches at Cushendun; one moment it's pouring, next it's time for ice cream; a Belfast doggie-turned-model waits for its moment in the sun; double rainbows; celebrating at an Irish concert.

From Cushendun to Slieve Donard

This poor wee man was out for a leisurely stroll in the park with his dog when we decided his Sheltie coordinated with my knitted coat. It took half an hour to encourage our four-legged friend to wear the coat, then it rained—and we waited another half hour to get the photo, but it was worth it. Dog and master loved the attention from their fellow dogs and masters who weren't getting to be stars.

Don't let the cottage parlor at Cushendun fool you—we were organized, honestly! Karen is knitting the collar for the mohair/linen coat while looking out to Cushendun Beach. When the rain stopped, everyone went back to Ballintoy Harbor to finish a shoot that was rained out the day before, and I stayed behind to finish an outfit.

Then we had to pack the car, as this was our last day there. Everything seemed to have expanded (including us, after having too much traditional Irish stew, cooked for us by Chef Stevie the night before).

Oh yes! While they were away and I was working in the living room looking out at the huge waves of the sea, lo and behold, something I have never seen in my life appeared: a double rainbow! I was so excited and didn't know if they could see it where they were—but leave it to Alexis to get the shot!

Then it was on to Newcastle, a town I visited many times as a young girl with my mum and dad, but it was only for a few hours, as we always had to get back to milk the cows.

The rain kept falling, and we were so thankful that the Slieve Donard Hotel—with its 120 bedrooms, Chippendale furniture, dazzling chandeliers, plush Persian carpets, and warm, friendly restaurant-bar—opened its doors for us (see photo, page 100). We made ourselves at home. The Slieve Donard's grand ballroom—with its bright conservatory—became our studio.

After a day of shooting, we were ready for a night off. They all wanted to hear and see some Irish music being played. To be sure, the luck of the Irish was with us when, by chance, Christie Moore was playing for two nights at the Slieve Donard Hotel. The concert was sold out, but while we were shooting I met Christie's manager and pleaded for tickets for my American comrades to see the show.

So with a glass of wine or beer, a bit of foot-tapping was done. Here was Christie Moore—one of Ireland's most renowned singers—and were my US guests even able to understand him? I had them in training.

(From top)
Titanic Memorial outside Belfast City Hall (the ill-fated ship was built in Belfast); medieval city gate and street sign in Londonderry.

to other countries for cheaper foreign labor. No more flax was grown in Ireland."

"What a lovely man, what a touching story," says author Maggie Jackson. "Living in Northern Ireland means you've been brought up with linen. And working on this book feels like I'm going back to my roots—linen is so much part of our history. It's so lucky to be able to use something in your work that's on your doorstep. Linen drapes so beautifully, you feel special when you wear it, and people love its natural color.

" 'They're not going to like our natural yarns,' I thought when I first came to Stitches East and saw all that wonderful color. All we offered in our stand was natural linen knitting kits in our trademark triangular boxes with rope handles, and handmade buttons.

"There I was, worried, and here comes this guy, happy-Larry, onto my stand with his camera clicking away, taking photographs. On most exhibitions at home you cannot take photographs of someone's work unless you have permission from the exhibitor or the organizer of the show. 'I'm sorry,' I said, 'you're not allowed to take photographs on this stand unless you have permission from myself or the organizers.' "

" 'Oh, I'm Alexis,' he said. 'I don't care *who* you are,' I said, 'you can't take pictures unless you have permission from the organizers.' 'It's OK, I'm XRX,' he said. 'I don't know who XRX is,' I said, 'you'll have to get permission from the Stitches people.' When, later, I asked at the Stitches booth who Alexis and XRX were, I was horrified. I was so new to the knitting universe I didn't know who anybody was—and thought I'd never get invited back again!"

But she was, and now XRX is with her in the van, along with cases of camera equipment, bags of garments, and lots of rain gear and umbrellas. May was proving to be unseasonably wet; in fact, it was turning into the wettest May ever. Still, we couldn't let a patch of bad weather discourage us, so here we were, speeding north toward the Antrim Coast, and Nuala.

"I've been working with Maggie for 21 years and thought I would do anything for her," says Irish beauty Nuala Meenehan. "But stand on that wee bridge, over that chasm? Never! Despite my loyalty, I just couldn't do it; I was too frightened.

"But then I thought how important this shoot was, how far you all had come. I looked at Maggie's face and I could see, 'Come on, Nuala, let's do it.' So I forgot my fear of heights—and walked."

In high-heeled boots, black leather pants, black tweed sweater, and hat—onto the swaying Carrick-a-rede Rope Bridge. Usually, this lacy link provides access to a tiny salmon-fishing island—but not today. The stormy weather that greeted our arrival in Ireland threatens to close it, as it did yesterday. Still, tourists in bright green, blue, and yellow rain gear, lined up to have their pictures taken, are waiting patiently in the mist as our XRX photo crew blocks the bridge.

"Hello, Rick?" *Knitter's* Editor Rick Mondragon, along as our stylist—under layers of sweaters and plastic ponchos—is recognized by one of his Stitches students. Will wonders never cease? Will the wind ever stop blowing? Will the rain please go away?

Well, no. But even in the mist, Carrick-a-rede is an amazing place, one of the jewels in the crown of The National Trust (see photo, page 139). Against the dark green of the coast and deep blue of the Irish sea, the bridge's airy rope network glistens like so much linen—perfect for Maggie's book.

"Three seconds before, I was thinking, 'I'm going to die!' " Nuala says. "But I held onto the ropes for dear life, trying to forget my fear, go on with the job. That's a picture that's never going to happen again!"

No need to, Nuala. With Carrick-a-rede's sweeping heights and soaring gulls we have our cover. Then it's time to walk back up the hill, another kilometer back to our van, and head to our next stop up the coast, magical Mussenden Temple. Black clouds fill the sky and the rain continues as we walk the two kilometers from Bishop's Gate to the Temple, a route that takes us through a well-fertilized sheep pasture. Thankfully, the Temple's huge door opens, and we can keep dry under its cavernous dome. This round folly, constructed in 1785, clinging precariously to a cliff on the Antrim Coast, becomes our sanctuary for the next few hours as the rain continues. Nuala, a busy advertising executive, keeps looking at her watch.

"I've been working with Maggie for two decades," she says. "It was one of my very first modeling jobs, and I was intimidated, but Maggie's enthusiasm put me at ease. I loved wearing her clothes as much then as I do now. I had never seen anything like her collection: so different, so beautiful, so comfortable. Quite simple stitches, really, yet such intricate-looking garments. Maggie adds bits of denim and leather that give her work not only the Maggiknits look, but a great street look. I hope knitters enjoy her work as much as I have enjoyed wearing her designs—and occasionally knitting them."

Dark cloud is followed by darker cloud, and the rain keeps falling, as it did all day yesterday at Cushendun, where outside our cozy seaside cottage the North Channel churned, and inside Maggie put finishing touches on her garments. Can you imagine sandy beaches, a great knit-wear collection, a beautiful model—and not being able to shoot? It was maddening. "I felt for you all," says Shannon Brown, a stunning redhead sidelined with us by the mist. "To wait around all day only to hear you say, 'Let's do it!'—at 6 p.m.! I tried my best to smile in that lacy vest, but I was so cold—all I wanted to do was go back inside and have a cup of tea.

"I did my very first photo shoot for Maggie when I was sixteen. Knitting, to a teenager like me, was something boring, something you had to learn in school. But Maggie's garments had an unusual, fun, Celtic feel about them. Come to think of it, Nuala was there on my very first shoot! How is she doing, by the way?"

Waiting for the rain to stop. A short break in the weather brings Nuala and our crew out into the open for a few glorious shots framed by Mussenden Temple. Then it is time to speed on to nearby Ballintoy Harbor with Nuala as our navigator. But the ten-minute trip down the coast turns into an hour-and-a-half of inland twists and turns, and we realize that we had taken one turn too many. By the time we make it to Ballintoy, a waterfall cascades down the cliff where none had been the previous day (see page 131). Nuala explains that no one in Northern Ireland looks at a map, and she offers to work late.

"I was worried about you all," Maggie says. "I knew Nuala had to be back at Belfast at 4:30, and here it was 8 p.m. and you were not back. I thought you must have gotten lost—or gone over a hedge!"

Actually, we had gone into the only dry place we could find in all of Northern Ireland, a cave. So we could keep shooting—in the rain. It was dark when we said our goodbyes to Nuala.

"It was my birthday!" says Nuala's husband, Jay Wyatt, laughing. "That's why Nuala wanted to come home early. But you all got caught up in the wildest, wettest spring on record."

Jay was on location at one of Maggie's early photo shoots. "It was on the shores of Belfast Lough, the main body of water that comes in from the Irish Sea," he says. "Lots of granite and stone on the banks and all these beautiful garments of Maggie's that seemed to have captured our entire Celtic tradition in a totally avant garde manner; it was mind boggling.

That wee rope bridge…

Alexis had Nuala terrified posing on that swaying bridge—so we made him take a dose of his own medicine and pose on that swaying bridge at Carrick-a-rede! Of course he had to pretend he was a model, changing clothes for the photo. You can't see us, but we're all under umbrellas—yet again!—in the background.

The rope bridge wobbles and twists as soon as you stand on it and only a couple of people are allowed on at one time. The island is a great bird sanctuary and visited by tourists from all over the world—as we discovered in trying to get them all off the bridge for our cover shot!

Nuala was afraid of heights, and this was her first shot. In high heels and leather pants, rain pouring down, her words were, "Only for you, Maggie," as Alexis had her stand 80 feet above the sea until he got his best shot.

The last time I was on the bridge, about five or six years ago, a shark had swum to our shores. When I looked down, all I could see was his fin, and I swore I would never go near the bridge again. Only for you, Alexis.

Traveling with XRX was a treat. They had enough suitcases for 20 people—we filled our large van; we filled the model's car; we filled our Cushendun landlady's home! So, of course, in Glenarm, Alexis decides to buy an antique settee for his puppies! Did he think of how he was getting it back to Belfast, never mind Sioux Falls? He managed with miles of bubble wrap and cardboard, but I will let him tell about trying to get this refrigerator-sized, odd-shaped package past customs.

And what can I say about our savior at the Ulster Folk and Transport Museum Lismacloskey Rectory? He fed us all Irish soda bread, wheaten bread, and David's favorite, treacle bread—all cooked on a griddle over an open fire. Treacle farls are cooked in a circle (like an old penny) then divided into quarters to represent a farthing (worth one fourth of a penny) and called a farl for short—Irish soda farls. Model Shannon could not get flour on her

outfit, so she had to be fed (see photo at left)!

The first day heading up the Antrim Coast, we didn't stop for food until near 3 o'clock. Well, it started being frustrating (Americans needing food!), then it got ridiculous—nothing was open. We had to laugh as I kept repeating, "This is not America."

The first two places we called at stopped serving at 2 p.m. (I had to explain to my friends there was no point in them serving food all afternoon when nobody was around—not holiday season yet.)

The next stop, after a few more miles, The Carnfurnock Country Park, had only one sandwich left.

The next place—Ballycastle Hotel—only served from 6 p.m. onwards. (This was not the Irish hospitality I had envisaged.)

Aah, at last (a sigh of relief on my part)—a signpost for the Drumnagreagh Hotel: "Food served all day." Lovely drive up the mountain, but it was closed! All out, not a sinner in sight!

Desperate and hungry, many miles later, we arrived in Glenarm at the Emporium Curio Café. The quaint little café at the back looked like we had walked into somebody's kitchen. The owner/cook was sitting with her feet up in front of the fire. She had just finished sending out 36 meals for people in homes. But she saw starvation on our faces and said she would get toasties and soup for us.

Now to me, customer service in the US is of a high standard—but this was Ireland. Our cook laid the napkins in a pile on the table and told us to fold them ourselves. She threw a handful of knives and forks down and we divide them out, then she pointed to the cupboard for us to get our own cups and saucers. She said she was getting on with the cooking! At this stage we more than wanted her in the kitchen and were happy to set the table ourselves.

We had a laugh and a great tea with apple tart and cream to follow, and smiles on our faces again! Only in Ireland. No 24-hour service here.

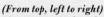

(From top, left to right)
No maps required; a photographer modeling at Carrick-a-rede; a local on the road to Ballycastle; soup and toasties in Glenarm; it all fits; finding a bargain at Charlie's Emporium Curio Cafe; tasting soda farls at the Ulster Folk and Transport Museum's Lismacloskey Rectory; lots of promises—but no food.

Jay, a lover of history, says, "The Celts expressed themselves through music, oral tradition, and more importantly, through patterns. You could say their whole way of life was written in those intricate, interlaced patterns. When I first saw Maggie's work I thought it was the embodiment of a tradition that was obviously deep within her heart, that she evolved and took forward in a contemporary way.

"*Maggie's Ireland* captures it all. The coastline, the ancient places, contemporary images that are tied to the earth and connected to an Ireland that is eternal and always. It's marvelous what she has done, under very difficult circumstances: we are not the center of the universe, and there was a war going on here."

"It was a difficult time," says Olive Clegg, who was Head of the Fashion Department at the Art College (now The University of Ulster) when Maggie was a student in the early 1970s. "We were based in the middle of Belfast, which obviously had a lot of problems at the time. We let our students go early because it wasn't safe on the street after dark."

The Troubles filled TV screens—and lives—with violence. And here was young Maggie, dreaming of the future. "I remember her very well," Mrs. Clegg says. "She had curly hair, and didn't have the punk image—pink hair or extreme clothes—a lot of students did. She wore fashionable, but sensible clothes and was very close to her family.

"She was a lovely person, a keen, enthusiastic, hard-working, talented student. She assisted me with teaching and everybody loved her, because she's always given a lot. Some designers hold something back—how they do things, how they succeed—because they don't want people to copy them. But Maggie always gave 100 percent.

"And she knew exactly what she wanted to do: she made up her mind that she wanted to be a knitwear designer. There really wasn't an awful lot of work for designers, as you can imagine, in Ireland as a whole, and certainly not in Northern Ireland. The option was to go to England or abroad, or else try to set up on your own here. Which was very difficult, because we didn't have the most favorable business climate.

"I tried to get the students away as much as possible—to Dublin, London, and Paris—and encouraged them to enter competitions. Our students' work was shown and compared with students' from further afield. And, of course, they'd travel to the exhibition.

"Maggie won some really big competitions in England. She had the ambition and she could pick up fashion wavelengths very easily and translate them into her work. We have a population of only a million-and-a-half people, and at that time it was quite rural. So it was difficult for any young person to advance themselves in the design field here. But Maggie was determined—she wanted to stay in Northern Ireland, and design. She's done well, I'm very proud of her. The only perk you get as a teacher is if your students do well.

"Because what we ran was a fashion course, our students studied the fashion trends and translated that 'look' into their work. Maggie managed to make the 'look' hers: elegant, formal knitwear, for what I call late-day occasions, for dressing up and looking smart, as well as for being casual—you could hike in some of her designs. She's selected the imagery that she likes and has kept it going. Like most good designers, she's managed to switch to whatever is fashionable, but keep the essence of her designs. Quite a clever thing to be able to do.

"When she first came to the school, I encouraged her to try different yarns and different stitches; to make them bigger and looser then do tight ones; to be exploratory in her approach. She started with what I would call 'craft knitting'—using basic techniques and basic stitches. Ireland is quite good for craft work and knitting, so she used that tradition, explored it, and then moved forward using linen.

"When you're setting up, you quite sensibly try to find something as your medium that is native to the way you live, something you're familiar with. Of course, linen was made in Northern Ireland, Maggie had access to it, and she exploited that medium. The manufacturers here were quite helpful and supportive, and obviously she found a market abroad.

"You often get talented students, but they've also got to have the

drive, the ambition—and good business sense. Maggie also brought up a family, three children… And the other thing that always amazed me is that she doesn't drive. She doesn't drive a car at all. If you live in a rural community, you don't have the greatest public transport, so how she got from A to B I will never know."

Well, Mrs. Clegg, let me tell you. Maggie remembers the way her family got places when she was young. Say you want her to direct you to Cushendun for your photo shoot? No problem—via Mossley, Milebush, Ballycarry, Glenoe, Glynn, Kilwaughter, Feystown, Glenarm, Glenariff, and Knocknacarry! A glance at the map will show that A26 and A44 take you directly to nearby Ballycastle—but, you guessed it, like Nuala, Maggie doesn't look at maps.

It was fun driving down all those winding country lanes—on the wrong side of the road. So what if we lost days to rain and hours to our non-map reader? The amazing sights more than made up for it. The countryside is so beautiful, so beguiling, that Northern Island's turbulent history is forgotten.

But Maggie remembers. "When I won that competition in London at the time of The Troubles," she says, "the designers from other colleges said, 'How can there be fashion coming out of Northern Ireland?' I wanted to prove to them that we could make something of ourselves."

Youthful ambition aside, what was it that made her think she could succeed?

"Madness! My parents wanted me to be a teacher—a nice, secure job. But I was young, enjoying the moment, working with fashion, fabrics, and yarns that I loved. Who's going to stop at seventeen and think where my customers are going to come from?

"I always made my own clothes. I started designing sweaters when I was twelve because I loved having something to wear that was different from anybody else's. Even in primary school we would hold a fashion show once a month. We would dress our Tressy dolls and pretend our desks were catwalks. Somebody would choose a winner, and we all took turns sampling the prize, a bar of chocolate.

"I must have been under seven when the vicar came to tea. My mum was very proud of her flowers (still is), and said to him, 'You must take a bunch of poppies for your wife.' But all that was left in the garden were the black balls in the center of the poppies! And there was my row of

(Clockwise from above)
Shamrocks and flowers at Mount Stewart; nobody's home so we sat on their hall furniture to rest, used their summer seat for a shot, then left as quietly as we had arrived—with everything back in its place.

The misty Mourne Mountains

The XRX team was surprised at all the yellow on the hills as they flew in. Of course, Alexis had to track it down. I know these plants as "whins." As a young girl, my brothers and I would put them in an old saucepan with water, over an open fire in a field, to boil eggs and dye their shells yellow. Then we would roll the eggs down the hill.

I knew I didn't want the XRX crew to stay in hotels, I wanted them to get a real feel for my Irish homeland. So I booked us into "Seaside Cottage" on the Antrim Coast and the "Millar's Close Cottages" at the foot of the Mourne Mountains, where there was even a cottage named "Maggie's." But it wasn't big enough for all of us, so we stayed next door in Rosie's. There was a view of the Mourne Mountains from every window and peat in the fireplace. (Rick and Alexis still don't agree who finally got that fire started.)

In our cottage in the Mourne Mountains—on the first night, preparing for the next day's shoot—I sewed (until 5:15 a.m.) in front of the peat fire so the model wasn't in knitwear and pins!

David sat by the fireplace with Irish coffee and laptop, Elaine ironed, Rick steamed, Karen went off to bed. We heard peals of laughter from her room and all rushed in to see Karen's bed in the far corner. She had jumped into bed and, as it was on wheels on a tiled floor, it flew across the room. Every time she laughed, she moved and the bed rolled off in a different direction, until Alexis anchored her ship of dreams with a dressing table!

Alexis would rise at dawn to wander and photograph to his heart's content, climbing fences, towers, and mountains, just to get the right shot.

Rain. Sun. Rain. Rain. Rain. Rain… Kate had had enough, waiting one-and-a-half hours for the sun to shine through the stained glass windows of the church—and we all had overindulged in sweets from the sweetie shop at the Ulster Folk and Transport Museum. But wasn't the photo worth the wait? (See page 91).

What you do for a book!

—Maggie Jackson

(From top, left to right) The green, green grass and hills of home; hairdressing in a farmer's front yard; 'Maggie's Cottage' in the Mourne Mountains; whiling away the hours at Rosie's Cottage—Elaine; Maggie; David; Rick; Karen; taking a break during a downpour. Stone walls—so much texture and earthy colors—how could a designer—or photographer—not be inspired? The Irish don't need maps—they have signposts; but that's another story…

dolls—sitting on the window ledge wearing red poppy-petal skirts, hats, and tops! I nearly got murdered.

"At the Art College I trained as a couturier designer, a tailor. I made suits and wedding dresses, and did a bit of knitting for my final collection in the third year. I enjoyed that very much. Then I did a post-graduate year specializing in fashion knitwear.

"Olive Clegg was the Head of the Fashion Department, and somebody you warmed to instantly. She had a very quiet manner, was English, well-educated, knowledgeable of international fashion. I felt a bond with her which grew over the years.

"I won a few competitions, and Mrs. Clegg—I still can't call her 'Olive,'—said, 'You've been on television, you've had some press, why don't you start your own business and see how it goes?'

"Initially, I had wanted to work for another designer, to learn more about the industry. But Mrs. Clegg told me, 'If you start in your own business now, if it doesn't work out, you're still young. Give it a couple of years and then go and work with another designer.'

"With her encouragement, I was the first designer to set up in Northern Ireland. It was quite a big step, because I didn't have anyone else to compare myself with or speak to. It was difficult: all of a sudden, you move from this happy, safe, secure environment of the school and you're on your own—in the big, deep world."

It's a new day, and Giant's Causeway awaits. But before we bid goodbye to Shannon, we must help repack her car. "It seems that everything expanded on this shoot," Maggie says. We stuffed all we could in Shannon's car, and still had to leave two bags of garments with our Cushendun landlady to be picked up another day.

Our van feels a little less crowded without the miniature, double-wide, Victorian settee we couldn't pass up at a local antique store—a present for XRX Mascots, Yorkies Violetta and Leonora. Does Maggie think she's got problems getting her garments through customs? If she only knew what we would go through trying to get this small-refrigerator-size package (that our packed settee turned out to be) through customs!

About an hour or so of driving along the magnificent Antrim Coast, Giant's Causeway stretched out before us, like the floating road of legend that spanned Ireland and Scotland—allowing giant Finn McCool to visit his lady love.

"Oh, Giant's Causeway!" Maggie says. "It was so wet, we tried to keep the rain away from our model with a giant umbrella. But how to keep the wind from blowing the garlic leaves we had picked at Mussenden Temple for our table settings?"

Table settings? "People talk a lot about Irish food," Maggie says, "and I thought perhaps a few recipes to get their minds away from potatoes and the famine would be good. The driver of the bus taking tourists down to the Causeway from the tourist pavilion kept saying, 'I've never seen so many photographs taken of food!'

We couldn't have done the shoot that day without that driver's help. He volunteered to stay after hours, carting our gear to and from the Causeway. "It was a sight not to be believed," Maggie says. "The wind was howling, scrims and reflectors were flying, cameras clicking; our model was looking magnificent; the photographer was yelling, 'Beautiful!' To the few onlookers who braved the weather to watch us work it must have seemed like something out of Hollywood.

"We also had my little grandson, Jake, with us—and all that food." Jake had made his modeling debut that morning, and now watched from his mother Kerrie's arms as his dad, Chef Stevie, arranged his food—and tried to keep those garlic leaves from flying away.

"Stevie, who has a passion for food, loved the idea," Maggie says, "but he was so nervous, he wanted everything to be just right. We bought dishes that would coordinate with the color theme of each section, and I knitted tablemats that tied in with the color themes. So we were prepared; the only thing we didn't know was where we were going to photograph. 'Are we going to shoot at a kitchen?' Stevie asked, and all I could say was, 'Expect the unexpected!' "

All those tan and brown, mostly hexagonal, basalt columns—by the thousands!—that make up this most unusual tourist attraction provided so many nooks and crannies for our table settings we didn't even bother looking for the Giant's Kitchen. And later that night, at Seaside Cottage, we feasted on a hearty Irish stew that Chef Stevie had prepared especially for us.

So it went, in Maggie's Ireland. Every turn, it seems, held a new surprise: a friendly ox with a fashionable hairdo (page 163); the ghostly outlines of historic Dunluce Castle clinging to the very edge of the land (page 160); the solitude of Silent Valley (page 161); the remains of Kinbane Castle slowly dissolving into the pounding sea (page 143); and, would you believe, a double rainbow (page 161).

"One day we drove around the corner, and there was the end of a rainbow in the middle of the road!" Maggie says. "Every time you get near a rainbow it moves further away from you. It seems we drove right through it. But we didn't have time to stop and look for the pot of gold, unfortunately, because our photographer wanted to get to his next shot.

Hard as it is to believe, not a single shot was taken of any of these wonders. The rain had made us so many days late, we thought we'd be lucky if we just got all Maggie's garments shot.

In Newcastle, at the foot of the Mourne Mountains, the rain still did not let up. When it did, it would only be for a few minutes—too little time to run outside, set up, and shoot a single frame.

But, for the first time, the weather did not matter—we had the elegant Slieve Donard Hotel at our disposal. The Donard's bright ballroom became our studio, but not before a hearty lunch at the four-star hotel's Art Deco bar. "What a blessing that was," Maggie says. "We were shooting evening clothes, and the hotel's sumptuous appointments suited the garments just fine. And that alcove window!"

The guests of the Slieve Donard—kept indoors by the inclement weather—gathered around our shoot. The bystanders included the stage crew and manager of Irish singer Christie Moore, who was kind enough to get us seats for that evening's sold-out show.

Then it was time to celebrate Rick's birthday in style—with a scrumptious Pavlova dessert made by Hilda Wells, a family friend. Maggie's short-sheeted bed added to the evening's excitement. "Oh, that night at 'Rosie's Cottage'—could you believe it?" says Maggie. "My knees hit my chin! And Karen got the giggles in bed and it starting rolling across the floor! But as Elaine said, 'If it was going to be a short night, might as well be in a short-sheeted bed!' "

There was also Irish coffee, a contest over who was the best at lighting a peat fire, and quiet time around the fireplace. "I was in old track bottoms," Maggie says, "no make-up, hair standing on end, and there was Alexis with the camera! But you promised me that picture is going to

(From top)
Portico of the Temple of the Winds at Mount Stewart; ornate lampost at Belfast City Hall.

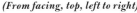

(From facing, top, left to right)
Two guards and one young model (posing with Shannon) at the Ulster Folk and Transport Museum; fancy hedge; scone, donut, tea or coffee?; off to school; a Greyabbey cornice becomes a planter; photographer's assistants hard at work; the soft light of a kerosene lamp; "She stayed so long," Maggie says, "they named a street after her"; keeping an eye on the shoot—Maggie's Ireland.

ELAINE STREET

"In 1993 I was chosen for an entrepreneurial program that would take me to Boston. But there were the kids…'We'll take them for four months,' my parents told me. 'This is a fantastic opportunity for you.' They could see I had lost my focus, my get-up-and-go, my confidence, and felt this all-paid trip to the US could put me on track again.

"My placement in Boston was at Neiman Marcus, where I was able to see how designers like Donna Karan and Armani were being marketed. I also studied international marketing and management at Boston College. It was an absolutely fantastic experience.

"In the course of my study, I had to get a business plan together, and could see that knitting and other crafts were quite popular in the United States. I came home with the idea that I could re-start my business in a totally new way—I would spend more time designing and selling internationally, focusing on boutiques, not individual clients. And I would market knitting kits.

"It was scary starting again from nothing. It took us about a year to get going, and in three years we were doing quite well.

"That's when we came to Stitches East. And the next three days took us by storm. We were shocked: some knitters even had heard of us. Knitting was a dying art at home, so you can imagine us coming back and telling everybody about American knitters! It was a totally different scene in the US, so unexpected. We were excited to have Trendsetter Yarns launch Maggiknits in the US. After two years we set up an office in New York. But commuting to the Big Apple from Ireland, traveling, doing workshops and exhibitions all over the world, and keeping an eye on the production back home allowed me less and less time to design. Knitting Fever offered me a golden opportunity: a Maggiknits yarn collection with accompanying design books.

"I love being in what you call 'the knitting universe,' bringing fashion to the knitter and showing that you, too, can produce a garment that's unique, exciting. I think of myself as a fashion designer who designs knitwear, and I look at the shape as opposed to the techniques—which are very simple. It gives me great pleasure to have a knitter say, 'I never thought I could knit something like this.' Or, 'It's the first time my husband noticed what I'm wearing in thirteen years!'

"My work is all about simple stitches for the average knitter. They're fun garments, fun to knit. As I'm knitting, I change the stitches as I go along because if I find it interesting, knitters will find it interesting. If I find it boring, they will too, and never finish it. My aim is for them to finish the garment—and look like a million dollars in it.

"In designing, I consider the total look. Even a casual sweater has to have sophistication. Look at the 'Connemara' sweater (in front of the Tea Room red door, page 14): the skirt is a simple two-two rib. The top is seed stitch on large needles. An openwork ladder-stitch section follows, then you continue with seed stitch, but in mohair. A beginner could knit it. You hear, 'I could never wear that ribbed skirt, I'm too fat.' But the longer-line sweater hides the hip line—it's actually very slimming.

"I love the styles from the 1920s to the 1940s—Erté, Edith Head, shoulder pads, uneven hems, garments that are comfortable, fun. The dipped, stepped hem in my designs—from small to large size—is very slimming. Mrs. Clegg taught me to 'make it good for the eye as well as the body.' There's no need to over-design. I tended to put everything in but the kitchen sink! Less is more.

I 'tone' a sweater rather than add more colors. Look at 'Peatland Cardi,' (page 112), the black tweed winter jacket. Toning is lifting the tan out of the tweed and emphasizing it in the garment—in the middle band and in the knitted tubes in the sleeves. The tubes have become one of our signatures. They're simple to do and give a three-dimensional look.

stay in your camera, right? I was up until 5 a.m. trying to finish off a garment, to make sure we had it for our shoot the next day."

Maggie has always been finishing things—even in the car on the way to a date: "I wanted to have a new outfit to impress my boyfriend," Maggie says, smiling, "and I'd be sewing on buttons in the car. 'Please, Mum, slow down. Take the long way, I've got to finish this hem!' I got married soon after graduating from Art College, so within the same month I became a wife and a work-from-home designer. Since I had been on television and in the papers I thought the designer part was going to be easy. I made the rounds of boutiques and shops with my knitwear collection thinking that they would buy from me. But I came back in tears, went out in the field amidst the cows, sat down, and cried some more.

"But inside, something told me, 'You can do it.' That's when I held a fashion show at a local hotel. Mum made the pastry and sandwiches for 300 people. When I look back, the affair was so country-yokel: my friends modeled, and I was in the back dressing them. We had about 60 outfits in the show and some of them weren't even finished, they were stuck together with double-sided sticky tape! But nobody noticed, we got orders, and that was the start of my private clientele.

"What an experience that was! You were working from home so they considered you a wee home knitter, a dressmaker—and you, working with expensive fabrics and yarns, were trying to make them think you were a fashion designer.

"They also thought you were a surgeon. People would come and say, 'I want something to hide the fact that I have one hip (or arm) higher than the other.' Or, 'Something to hide my arms, my neck.' I realized then that no one feels that her body is 100% superb—we all want to disguise something. So I started designing garments that would look good on everybody—slim to large.

"In 1989 I became a single parent with three small children, and that was difficult. I was making ready-mades for people, one-off designs. My workers did the basic knitting, but I did the embellishments and detailing myself. It was time-consuming: I'd come home in time to get the children to bed around 9:30 p.m., and be up until one or two in the morning.

"I had bought a one-room schoolhouse near my house, and I was pushing an old pram and a couple of bags of knitting up the hill, because I never drove. I was always walking.

"In 1991 I had to close my business because of illness; I nearly died of peritonitis. That was a hard time. The stress had taken its toll; I was burned out. I didn't look at knitting—something I had loved since I was six years old—for two years. I had always focused on where I was going, and now I had lost my direction.

(Clockwise from above)
Circular stairway, round tower and abbey ruins at Devenish Island; turning Giant's Causeway's polygonal niches into a set for Chef Stevie's food.

(Facing page, right to left)
Maggie's Ireland Calendar; and the endless road—the trip of a lifetime.

"With *Maggie's Ireland*, I feel that I'm going back to my roots as a designer. And the same is true of the linen. With linen I have been able to come up with something that is different."

And her signature splits?

"They're my way to bring color to the design. You can knit these sections separately, without carrying yarns across the back. It's so much fun to have these splits—they give my garments such a different look. They even remind me of my first knitting, it was so full of holes my mum despaired."

Speaking of desperation, "My poppies! I went out to get Reverend Larmour some flowers, and they were all gone," says Maggie's mother, Sylvia. "Maggie was always good with her hands. She was like a wee granny knitting away in the corner. Her father and I discouraged her from becoming a designer. We thought teaching would be a steadier job. But she's a very determined person. If Maggie got a notion in her head, you couldn't have turned her, she ran away with it. But I'm sure you've found this out yourself?"

Is Sylvia talking about our long discussions in the car, when the map said one thing, Maggie another? But there's no time to find out. Sylvia is holding a huge Pavlova, a birthday dessert made for Rick by family friend Hilda Wells, and we've got hours to go to get to the Mourne Mountains— even following the map.

In the car heading south, Maggie says, "Mum asked how the photos turned out. I told her I cried when I saw them. 'Where they that bad?' she said. 'No, they were that good,' I replied. I'm so happy to have Northern Ireland be the backdrop of my book. It was two weeks of long, hard work, but so satisfying. It's something that will stay with me the rest of my life.

"And the luck of the Irish *was* with us—that little Sheltie that showed up at the park just when we needed it to model the doggie coat; the Slieve Donard that kept us dry in that cataclysm; all those double rainbows!

"I'm so glad you've loved Northern Ireland, rain and all. I have waited 25 years to show the world how beautiful my country is—and that we've survived The Troubles and the fear."

When most of our crew returned home, Elaine and I stayed behind: *Maggie's Ireland* beckoned—and the sun was supposed to come out.

—*Alexis Xenakis*
Sioux Falls, South Dakota

While in Ireland, you won't want to miss the National Trust's Carrick-a-rede, Downhill Estate (that includes Mussenden Temple), Giant's Causeway, and Mount Stewart (House, Garden, and Temple of the Winds); Dunluce and Kinbane Castles; the Ulster Folk and Transport Museum outside Belfast; The Irish Linen Centre & Lisburn Museum in Lisburn; Eugene McConville's scutching mill in Dromore (011 44 289 269 2512); the Silent Valley and Mourne Mountains; the Antrim Coast; Lower Lough Erne's Devenish and Boa Islands; and, at Castle Archdale Marina (near Irvinstown) ask for Captain Mickey—give him our love, and ask him to ferry you to White Island and its eerie stone faces.

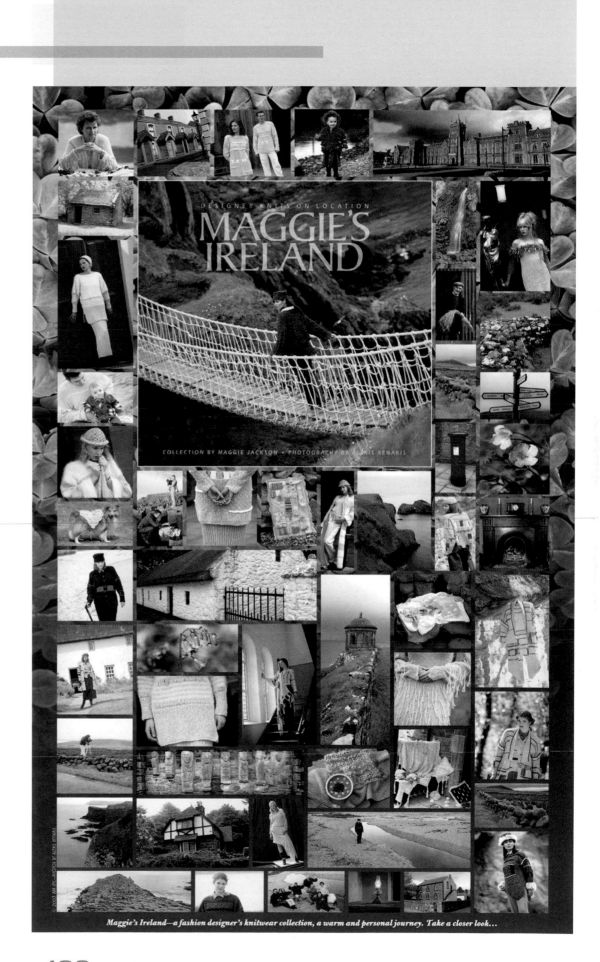

Maggie's Ireland—a fashion designer's knitwear collection, a warm and personal journey. Take a closer look...

Cable Cast-On

Uses A cast-on that is useful when adding stitches within the work.

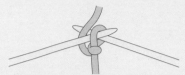

1 Make a slipknot on left needle.

2 Working into this knot's loop, knit a stitch and place it on left needle.

3 Insert right needle between the last 2 stitches. From this position, knit a stitch and place it on left needle. Repeat Step 3 for each additional stitch.

I-Cord

I-cord is a tiny tube of stockinette stitch, made with 2 double-pointed needles.

1 Cast on 3 or 4 sts.
2 Knit. Do not turn work. Slide stitches to opposite end of needle. Repeat Step 2 until cord is the desired length.

Ladder stitch

1 K1, wrapping yarn 2 or more times around needle.

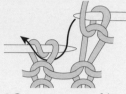

2 On next row, purl into stitch, dropping all the wraps.

SSK

Uses A left-slanting single decrease.

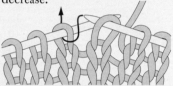

1 Slip 2 sts separately to right needle as if to knit.

2 Knit these 2 sts together by slipping left needle into them from left to right; 2 sts become one.

Tassels

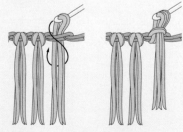

1 Insert crochet hook through a stitch. Draw center of strands through, forming a loop.
2 Draw ends through loop. One tassel complete.

Wrap & Turn for Short Rows

Uses Each short row adds two rows of knitting across a section of the work. Since the work is turned before completing a row, stitches must be wrapped at the turn to prevent holes. Work a wrap as follows:
Knit side

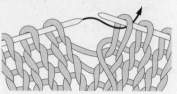

1 With yarn in back, slip next stitch as if to purl. Bring yarn to front of work and slip stitch back to left needle as shown. Turn work.

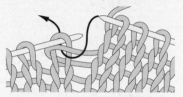

2 When you come to the wrap on the following knit row, make it less visible by knitting the wrap together with the stitch it wraps.

Yarn Over Between Purls

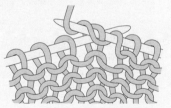

With yarn in front of needle, bring yarn over needle and to front again, purl next stitch.

Use the charts and guides below to make educated decisions about yarn thickness, needle size, garment ease, and pattern options.

YARN WEIGHT CATEGORIES

Yarn Weight

1	2	3	4	5	6
Super Fine	*Fine*	*Light*	*Medium*	*Bulky*	*Super Bulky*

Also called

Sock	Sport	DK	Worsted	Chunky	Bulky
Fingering	Baby	Light-	Afghan	Craft	Roving
Baby		Worsted		Aran	Rug

Stockinette Stitch Gauge Range 10cm/4 inches

27 sts	23 sts	21 sts	16 sts	12 sts	6 sts
to	to	to	to	to	to
32 sts	26 sts	24 sts	20 sts	15 sts	11 sts

Recommended needle (metric)

2 mm	3.25 mm	3.75 mm	4.5 mm	5.5 mm	9 mm
to	to	to	to	to	to
3.25 mm	3.75 mm	4.5 mm	5.5 mm	8 mm	16 mm

Recommended needle (US)

1 to 3	3 to 5	5 to 7	7 to 9	9 to 11	13 to 19

Locate the Yarn Weight and Stockinette Stitch Gauge Range over 10cm/4" on the chart. Compare that range with the information on the yarn label to find an appropriate yarn. These are guidelines only for commonly used gauges and needle sizes in specific yarn categories.

FIT

VERY CLOSE FIT

actual bust/chest
or less

CLOSE FIT

bust/chest
plus 1-2"

STANDARD FIT

bust/chest
plus 2-4"

LOOSE FIT

bust/chest
plus 4-6"

OVERSIZED FIT

bust/chest
plus 6" or
more

MEASURING

- **A** Bust/Chest
- **B** Body length
- **C** Center back to cuff
  (arm slightly bent)

CONVERSION CHART

centimeters		0.394		inches
grams		0.035		ounces
inches	X	2.54	=	centimeters
yards		.91		meters

GLOSSARY

US	UK
bind off	cast off
seed stitch	moss stitch
gauge	tension
stockinette stitch (St st)	stocking stitch
work even	work straight
yarn over (yo)	yarn forward, yarn over needle, or yarn round needle

SIZING   Measure around the fullest part of your bust/chest to find your size.

Children	6mo	18mo	2	4	6	8	10
Actual chest	17"	19"	21"	23"	25"	26.5"	28"

Women	XXS	XS	Small	Medium	Large	1X	2X	3X
Actual bust	28"	30"	32–34"	36–38"	40–42"	44–46"	48–50"	52–54"

Men	Small	Medium	Large	1X	2X
Actual chest	34–36"	38–40"	42–44"	46–48"	50–52"

YARNS *from* MAGGI'S MK COLLECTION

Maggi's Faux Fur
Beige, grey, black; Man-made materials

Yarns from Maggi's Collection are available at fine yarn shops everywhere and from your favorite shops online at **StitchesMarket.com**

Maggi's Tweed Fleck Aran *Olive, charcoal, black*
Wool tweed; 3½ oz/100g; 153yds/140m; Medium weight
Maggi's Tweed Fleck Chunky *Denim, beige, cerise*
Wool tweed; 3½ oz/100g; 120yds/110m; Bulky weight

Maggi's Mohair *Black, navy, ivory, denim blue; Mohair, wool, nylon; 1¾ oz/50g; 110yds/99m; Bulky weight*

Maggi's Merino Aran *Camel, pale grey, black; Merino wool; 1¾ oz/50g; 85yds/77m; Medium weight*

Maggi's Linen *Natural, navy, olive, chocolate, mustard, black, cream, white; Cotton, linen; 1¾ oz/50g; 126yds/113m; Medium weight*

Maggi's Mist Slub *Beige/grey, beige/red, beige/olive; Viscose; 1¾ oz/50g; 88yd/80m; Medium weight*

Maggi's Denim *Light blue, mid blue, dark blue; Cotton; 1¾ oz/50g; 50yds/45m; Bulky weight*

Maggi's Metallic *Silver, gold, bronze; Acrylic, cotton, nylon, polyester; 1¾ oz/50g; 88yds/80m; Medium weight*

Maggi's Ribbon *Navy, black, ivory, white; Nylon; 1¾ oz/50g; 99yds/89m; Bulky weight*

Maggi's Rag Yarn *Denim, olive, chocolate, white, red, tan; Cotton, acrylic, polymide; 1¾ oz/50g; 69yd/63m; Bulky weight*

Special thanks to our models: Nuala, Shannon, Kate, Kathryn, Pauline, Robert, and, not forgetting the kids, Emmer, Timmy, and Jake. You were an important part of the team.

Maggie's Ireland—it started with beautiful, natural-fiber yarns, a large collection of designs, and many questions: *Do the garments look good? Will somebody really wear them? Is it knitting without anxiety? Will it motivate a knitter? Does it have ideas readers can adapt for their age or size? Will they feel like a million dollars?* If the answers, readers, are 'yes' and if I have convinced you to visit my beautiful, now-peaceful country, then I have accomplished something very important.

Many people have made it possible. Where do I start? It has to be with my mum, an avid knitter in her youth, who passed her skills on to me. Her constant and dedicated love, support, and help in meeting deadlines go far beyond duty. If I am half the mother that you have been to me, then my kids are lucky indeed. My gratitude is boundless.

To my dad—for all the years of helping me plan and create displays, accessories, anything to forward my career. Love you and miss you.

To my three children—Simon, Kerrie, and Jodie—for tolerating yarn in every room and mohair in your food.

To the staff at XRX in Sioux Falls, you made me feel like one of your team, for your enthusiasm and support of the book.

To the XRX photo crew—Alexis, David, Elaine, Karen, and Rick—who, on your trip to Ireland through rain, hailstones, injury, and miles of walking, brought Northern Ireland and my designs together for this presentation.

But pictures and words do not make a book—someone must put them all together, and for that I thank Bob Natz's talent and Elaine's vision. Making editorial sense of an avalanche of patterns and photographs is a challenge indeed; they couldn't do it without Nancy, Sue, Denny, Carol, Jay, Ev. . . .

I cannot give enough praise to a very special, genius photographer—Alexis. His conscientiousness, determination, and innovation through bad weather, injury, and driving on the wrong side of the road (and will he let me forget it?!) culminated in photographs that brought tears of joy to my eyes. Words don't say enough— the photos do! I love him to bits.

Special thanks for our homes on the road: Malone House in Belfast (Ruby, you're the best), Seaside Cottages at Cushendun, and Mourne Mountain Cottages. To Eugene McConville; Ulster Folk and Transport Museum, Cultra, County Down, and the children from Kilkeel Primary School; the Irish Linen Centre & Lisburn Museum, Lisburn, County Antrim; Slieve Donard Hotel and their staff, Newcastle, County Down; and to my knitters and staff over the years.

—*Maggie*